Sue Patton Thoele's books have long been a guiding light for me. *The Mindful Woman* is warm, wise, and wonderful and has become a touchstone to which I turn for advice and clarity. Reading Sue Thoele has truly made a difference in my life and has made me more mindful of the happy, healthy woman I am becoming.

—Brenda Knight, author of *Wild Woman and Rituals for Life*

A wise, witty, and wonderful guide to what eludes us most: peace of mind and heart in a turbulent world.

—Janice Lynne Lundy, author of *Your Truest Self*

…A mixture of awareness, meditation, and positive psychology, with a stiff helping of Buddhist "non-attachment" [*The Mindful Woman*] should speak powerfully to women of all faiths.

—Library Journal

This book now has a permanent place on my nightstand. *The Mindful Woman* does much more than inform the reader about mindfulness. Through tiny, sweet bites of easy practice, it transforms a thoughtful woman into a mindful woman. Sue Patton Thoele's tenderness toward her reader warms each page as she reveals her own slips and slides in finding the positive and pleasant view of every circumstance.

—Cynthia Wall, LCSW, author of *The Courage to Trust*

the
mindful
woman

gentle practices for
restoring calm, finding balance
& opening your heart

SUE PATTON THOELE

New Harbinger Publications, Inc.

Publisher's Note

This publication is designed to provide accurate and authoritative information in regard to the subject matter covered. It is sold with the understanding that the publisher is not engaged in rendering psychological, financial, legal, or other professional services. If expert assistance or counseling is needed, the services of a competent professional should be sought.

Distributed in Canada by Raincoast Books

Copyright © 2008 by Sue Patton Thoele
New Harbinger Publications, Inc.
5674 Shattuck Avenue
Oakland, CA 94609
www.newharbinger.com

Cover design by Amy Shoup; Cover image: Charles Krebs/Botanica/Jupiterimages; Text design by Amy Shoup and Michele Waters; Acquired by Melissa Kirk; Edited by Carole Honeychurch

---

Library of Congress Cataloging-in-Publication Data

Thoele, Sue Patton.
   The mindful woman : gentle practices for restoring calm, finding balance, and opening your heart / Sue Patton Thoele.
      p. cm.
   Includes bibliographical references (p.   ).
   ISBN-13: 978-1-57224-542-6 (pbk. : alk. paper)
   ISBN-10: 1-57224-542-5 (pbk. : alk. paper)
   1. Peace of mind. 2. Women--Psychology. I. Title.
   BF637.P3T52 2008
   158.1082--dc22

                              2008002249

FSC
MIX
Paper
FSC® C011935

15   14   13

10   9   8   7   6   5

To my heart-daughters,
Paige, Lynnie, and Colleen,
who are among my most potent teachers and dearest loves.

contents

acknowledgments

*W*hat a pleasure it has been to work with the wonderful people from New Harbinger Publications. To Julie Bennett, who rescued my first book from the slush pile and, more recently, rescued me from retirement and lured me back into the writing world that I love so much. And to Melissa Kirk and Jess Beebe, who respond quickly and kindly and threw great ideas in the creative cauldron. To Carole Honeychurch, who edits with sure and gentle hands and an understanding heart. To Troy DuFrene, Heather Mitchener, Michele Waters, and Amy Shoup, who made this book so much more accessible and appealing. Thank you all.

Thanks and hugs to Judith Mangus, soul sister, whose wisdom lures me into some pretty weird places. Much gratitude to Laura Jahanara Mangus, whose teachings continually center my heart. To Sonja, who is unfailingly compassionate. To the WOWs, Jean, Kamilla, and Linda, who provide ballast and much needed laughter. To Mary, Jane, Jean Marie, and Daune, and all the women of the Quest group, who anchor my weeks with listening and learning. To Susan, Karen, and Bonnie, and all the other women whom I do and will love. You are my cornerstones.

As always, heartfelt thanks to my in-house family. Gene, who keeps me laughing and is my rock, wings, and favorite playmate. In this book, more than any other, he has been an invaluable collaborator, feeding me articles, quotes, and ideas that enriched the final product immeasurably. Lily, the cutest most appealing dog in the universe, who keeps me smiling. And Riley, the sweetest most beautiful cat ever, who keeps me humble by creating lots of boogers, litter, and hair for me to clean up.

Resounding thanks to my out-of-house family, Mike, Paige, Chad, Lynnie, Shawn, Josh, Alex, Grant, and Caitlin, who are not only patient with the absences writing creates but also provide a loving support system at all times. And Brett and Colleen, thank you for knowing firsthand the tedium and exhilaration of writing, and holding my hand during both.

To my faithful and gentle muses, unending gratitude...

an ongoing adventure

I am so excited to be writing *The Mindful Woman*. It's a blessing to have the opportunity to explore what a majority of us yearn for in our heart of hearts but easily lose sight of amid the whirl of everyday life: that women want peace of mind, open hearts, and an enduring sense of balance and purpose. We want to dispel fear with gratitude and joy. And we want to love ourselves as deeply and unselfishly as we do others. We want to matter and feel fulfilled.

Can learning to live mindfully grant us all those desires? I don't know, but I do know I feel a lot more peaceful, open-hearted, and well-balanced since discovering the promise and practice of mindfulness. Although I'm sure age and circumstances are factors in my softening toward myself and life in general, I'm continually amazed by the fun and joy that accompanies mindfulness ... when I remember to do it.

While I'm not an expert on mindfulness by any stretch of the imagination, I am passionately committed to increasing mindfulness in both my inner and outer journeys. I leaped at the chance to write this book because one of the best ways to learn something at a deep and enduring level is to teach it. However, in the process of trying to practice what I write, I'm alternately appalled and amused by just how elusive mindfulness can be, how incredibly easy it is for me to be seduced away from simplicity and focused awareness into multi-multitasking and rampant mind-mucking.

This morning provided a good example of doing too many things at once and, thereby, becoming absentminded rather than mindful. I caught myself stumbling over my credit card number while giving it to a catalog saleswoman because I was simultaneously bringing up my e-mails, scrubbing my allergic cat's boogers off my computer screen, and obsessing about how I was going to start this introduction. That was a harmless and amusing little episode, but others are not so funny. When I'm too exhausted to sleep because I'm overcommitted, obsessively worried, resentful, or trying to solve the woes of the world—or, more likely, those of my immediate family—that's not funny.

Thankfully, both science and psychology now recognize that the stress of busy mindlessness is epidemic in our society. Many more of us know from experience that unrelenting helter-skelter thoughts and behaviors can result in damaged health, poor relationships, and a chaotic mind, to name only a few harmful effects. Awareness is the first step in making positive change. Knowing that mindlessness creates harmful stressors, we can choose to turn toward mindfulness, which roots us deeply in the moment and plants us firmly in the reality of now. Mindfulness neutralizes inner and outer chaos and invites balance and harmony into our lives and beings.

Searching for the grace that comes with mindful living is an ongoing adventure. When grace holds my hand during comfortable times, I feel in the flow with all that is good and right within and around me, and life seems joyous, light, fun, and comforting. During difficult yet mindful times, life can feel rich, moist, and growth producing. So why are mindful times more rare than regular? Why do I too often feel the need to exhort myself to "Slow down! Shut up! Stay open!" in a manner that contradicts my long-term motto of "Live gently with yourself and others"?

I imagine mindful times are rarer than I would like because my energy is jangled and scattered, my awareness snagged on the past or the future—a fragment in the bread aisle of the supermarket, a slice gnawing on a bothersome remark by a coworker, a smudge on the malfunctioning computer, a wedge worried about an upcoming deadline or a struggling adult child. In other words, when I'm not inhabiting my life right now, there's no place for balance, harmony, and grace to stick. Now is the only time anything truly exists. Right now—this moment, this experience, this feeling, this interaction—is our life. All else is shadow and smoke.

Consciously living in the moment is at the core of mindfulness practices. Being mindful is being truly alive. Mindfulness allows you to be fully present to your authentic self and to live your life with acute awareness and an open heart. Does this mean you may experience pain more deeply? Possibly. Will mindfulness bring you more joy and serenity? Yes, I've found that to be true. Is it worth the effort? For me, absolutely. Because you are reading this, my bet is you already have tasted the depth, meaning, and magic of mindful living and would love to experience more of it in your busy life.

My intention and dream for *The Mindful Woman* is that it defines mindfulness in an easily understood way, provides stories and examples of women who find mindful living rewarding, and gives you many practices that can make the path easier and more fun, should you choose to pursue it. My heart will sing if *The Mindful Woman* provides a springboard for both you and me from which we can dive openheartedly into the numinous now and live our lives more fully, joyously, and consciously. I hope the stories included in the book not only inspire you but also make you feel as if you have friends along the way. They show that I, and all the women portrayed, lurch, stumble, fall, and forget a thousand times, but the beautiful feelings of peace, joy, relaxation, and openheartedness that mindfulness brings keep us recommitting to the journey.

The Mindful Woman can be used in a variety of ways—as a meditation guide, a daily friend and reminder, or the answer to a specific question. Part 1 explores the basics of mindfulness and outlines many ways in which it enriches your life. Part 2 consists of stories, how-tos, and practices designed to help you restore calm, find balance, and open your heart by becoming more adept at mindfulness. Part 3 is a summation and celebration of the benefits to be enjoyed through mindful living. If you want to make one particular practice a habit, try concentrating on it for twenty-one days straight. Experts have found that it takes twenty-one days to either break an old habit or create a new one. You can also ask for the perfect, right entry for the moment and open the book at random. Random opening is intuitive and fun, and it sometimes elicits an amazed, "No way!" Or you may enjoy the process of moving through the book in sequence. Trust yourself and use *The Mindful Woman* in ways that speak to your heart in the moment. There is no right or wrong way to practice.

Although the myriad practices within these pages have helped other women create minutes of mindfulness and oases of awareness amid the hustle and hassle of everyday activities, they are by no means the be-all and end-all. You probably already know of, or will be drawn to create, exercises and practices specifically tailored to your desires and needs.

Each of us has the ability to nurture mindfulness in her own unique way. The peace of mind and heart gained from a mindful attitude is well worth the commitment. Mindfulness helps us love ourselves more gently and completely. Wrapped in the comfort and security of self-love, our hearts naturally open, and love flows more freely to others. And love is the essence of all that matters.

part one

exploring the basics

chapter 1

what is mindfulness, and why do we want it?

Mindfulness means paying attention in a particular way; on purpose, in the present moment, and nonjudgmentally. —Jon Kabat-Zinn

*M*indfulness is being aware of yourself, others, and your surroundings in the moment. When consciously and kindly focusing awareness on life as it unfolds minute by precious minute, you are better able to savor each experience. Also, being closely attentive gives you the opportunity to change unwise or painful feelings and responses quickly. In fact, being truly present in a mindful way is an excellent stress reducer and, because of that, can be seen as conscious-ness conditioning, a strengthening workout for body, mind, heart, and spirit.

While few of us have the temperament, financial freedom, or life circumstances to allow long periods of meditation, extended retreats, or endless Zen walks, we *can* gather scat-tered energy and awareness by practicing mindful moments each and every day! In time, moments become minutes, and minutes ultimately become a more present and peaceful way of life.

Elements of Mindfulness

To make mindfulness more accessible to we busy women, I've highlighted four elements that I believe are essential in day-to-day practice. These are paying attention, living in the moment, simplifying, and breathing. There are, of course, numerous facets to each element of mindfulness, and we will explore many of them in part 2, The Practices.

1. Paying Attention

When you focus your awareness on someone or some-thing, you are paying attention. You have narrowed your field of vision and chosen to look at the person or thing through mental and emotional binoculars. The object of your atten-tion becomes your focal point. Focused attention allows you to see clearly and in finer detail. Interestingly, almost any person or thing to whom we pay close attention gains value in our hearts and minds. Concentrated awareness leads to better understanding of and appreciation for that which we are attentive to. For instance, truly listening to someone and hearing them at a meaningful level adds richness and depth to the relationship. By compassionately focusing your attention on another, it's possible to understand their thoughts, feelings, desires, and doubts more intimately. Deep understanding opens your heart. While the *un*known can feel threatening or suspicious, the *known* is more easily lovable. Very often, to know and understand another is to love them.

Attention is an invaluable gift to give.

When discussing mindfulness with my son Brett, he said, "I think the reason I love adrenalin-rush sports so much is that I *have* to stay present and pay attention. If I don't, it could be a matter of life or death." Just what a mother wants to hear, right? He does have a great point, however. While not paying attention to yourself may not catapult you off a mountain cornice to your doom or grind you into the sand beneath a monstrous wave, as it could my son, neglecting yourself over time is so wearing that you can lose your joy and enthusiasm for life. Lack of attention may not physically kill you, but having heard my own and many women's comments such as "This is killing me!" and "I feel empty and dead inside" and "I think this relationship [or job or stress] is sucking the life right out of me," I know that self-neglect is very harmful indeed.

Because paying loving attention often results in valuing, understanding, and enjoying what you pay attention to, it's incredibly important you place yourself at—or very near—the top of your pay-attention-to list. Just as knowing and understanding another often leads to loving them more fully, the same is true with yourself. Gently and lovingly paying attention to yourself offers you the opportunity to know, understand, and accept yourself more completely and, consequently, to fall in love with yourself just the way you are in this moment.

Another bonus received from paying close attention to ourselves and the moment at hand is that we recognize habits and behaviors that no longer add value and joy to our lives. Being conscious of counterproductive or self-sabotaging actions, reactions, and responses as they happen gives you the opportunity to stop and make a different choice, one that is more conducive to health and peace of mind. Focusing awareness on the now not only gives you the opportunity to change what isn't working, it also allows you to enhance and appreciate that which is working. Especially when feeling pressured or rushed, it's easy to circle the drain out of habit or fear, clinging to what is driving us crazy. Thankfully, mindful living leads to an intentional life that is *on purpose* and promotes calm, balance, and peace of mind and heart.

2. *Living in the Moment*

As a psychotherapist who believes much of our healing comes from understanding and forgiving the past, and as someone who loves to revisit wonderful experiences in order to revel in the feelings they elicited the first time around, I've struggled with the concept of continually living in the moment. What does living in the moment really mean? Where do planning for the future, scheduling appointments in advance, making reservations for a future trip, and all the other realities of life fit into the idea of living in the moment? How can living moment to moment complement my forays into the past and my need to stay sane by preparing for things to come?

I was talking Colleen, my "spiritual" daughter—chosen by my heart though not born of my body—about not having come to a satisfactory conclusion about living in the moment, when she said, "I've been thinking about that too and have decided that what I am *consciously* doing in the moment *is* the moment." Aha! The proverbial lightbulb went on, and living in the moment became a believable and doable objective. For me, "consciously" is the significant word here. As I understand it, when we consciously do, think, or experience something, our attention is fully engaged and we are connected to the reality of what is going on. Therefore, if we are consciously paying attention and aware of planning for the future or thinking of the past right here, right now, we are still living in the moment.

While I believe mindfulness can include understanding and savoring the past or planning, imagining, and envisioning the future, we will concentrate on the description given by long-term, renowned teachers who see mindfulness as being consciously, compassionately, and nonjudgmentally present to what is happening *now*. It's important to focus on staying in the moment because, although we can remain mindful of the here and now when we consciously project our thoughts into the future or decide to move back in time to review the past, it is incredibly easy to fall out of a mindful state when our thoughts switch to automatic pilot and skitter off in many directions.

Contrary to how it may sound, mindfulness is not arduous or overwhelming. In reality, mindfulness is calming, grounding, and centering. Nonetheless, I can still almost hear you gasping, as my friend Cynthia did, "What! How can I—multitasking wizard, perfectionist, codependent (always an ear, eye, or hand distracted toward other people's needs)—become a mindful woman?" The answer is simple, although not necessarily easy. We become mindful women through intentional practice, practice, practice.

I'm sure you've heard the saying "Take it one day at a time." While a day at a time is a great concept, we all know that one day may contain way too much for us to handle during certain circumstances like intense grief, physical pain, or fear. In soul-searing situations, taking it one minute or one breath at a time may be the most we can do. The same small-step principle works in your practices for becoming a more mindful woman. Take it one tiny, tolerant little step at a time. At least that's how I, and other women I know, are progressing toward increased mindfulness—one gentle, conscious moment at a time. In fact, the theme of *The Mindful Woman* is that a few mindful moments make a world of difference.

3. Simplifying

Even though therapists and spiritual teachers, including the Dalai Lama, assure us that simplifying our lives will make us happier, not only do many of us have plates full to overflowing, but we are also juggling several at once. As a result, our time and energy can become fragmented by trying to answer the braying demands of multiple obligations and opportunities. Because we are many things to many people, it's easy to be on call 24/7 to everyone else and forget ourselves. One of my clients explained her experience of obligation and being overwhelmed as feeling "nibbled to death by ducks."

Gently coaxing yourself back into the now by moving your attention away from the army of ducks seemingly poised for future attack and choosing to focus only on the ducks nibbling *in the moment* helps alleviate feelings of being overwhelmed. You can usually manage almost anything if you simplify by taking it one small step at a time, one little bite at a time ... moment by moment. I've found that making detailed lists is also a great help in implementing the small-step approach to almost anything. Of course, there are extraordinary times of exhaustion, illness, stress, or grief when the moment itself is so overwhelming that no amount of simplification helps. In those dire times, we need to allow others to carry us.

But, even in extreme situations, and definitely in day-to-day reality, mindful living helps us opt for the serenity of simplicity, the blessing of feeling *under*whelmed, and gives us the ability to recognize whatever comfort is available in the moment. Because mindful minutes calm our souls, quiet our minds, and open our hearts, they are well worth the effort of learning and incorporating them into our lives.

There are countless ways to simplify your inner and outer lives, and most of them bring at least a modicum of relief and relaxation. My friend Sonja, who recently retired, is now busily and happily simplifying her home by throwing out at least twenty-seven things a day and organizing to her heart's content. Her heart actually is more content. "All the clutter was affecting me physically and emotionally," she said enthusiastically. "I'm already feeling so much lighter and freer and *proud* of myself." With the luxury of time, Sonja is bringing more balance and harmony into her home and heart by getting rid of material things that are no longer necessary or helpful.

In the process of simplifying her physical space, Sonja is clearing and cleansing interior space as well. You may benefit from doing the same. If you have a habit of castigating yourself with derogatory self-talk, like "You dummy you!" it needs to be thrown out. Or perhaps you are lugging around an old grudge or injury that needs to be forgiven in order for love to flow freely from and to you. How much simpler our lives are when we toss such things in the trash and symbolically burn them into transformation.

Simple is calming. Simple is satisfying.

Simplifying creates inner and outer space; space invites serenity.

4. Breathing

Breath is the bridge between body and mind and the gateway to the present moment. By focusing on your breath, you can easily bring yourself into the here and now and attune mind and heart to your physical body. Many of the practices in part 2 focus on ways you can use breath to increase mindfulness and body awareness. Breath practices are centered around the following guidelines:

* Attention to breath

* Deepening of breath

* Directing the breath

Breathing is the first thing we do after birth and the last thing we do before death. Breath is life. Breath is a master teacher. Using your breath consciously and constructively enhances your vitality, increases daily joy, opens you more fully to love, and brings you richly and deeply into the practice of mindfulness.

Myths of Mindfulness

Having just explained how I view mindfulness and outlined the four elements we will be concentrating on in *The Mindful Woman*, I'd now like to highlight a couple of myths about mindfulness.

Myth 1: Mindfulness Is Meditation

While mindfulness and meditation do bring similar benefits and both are intended to quiet and center body, mind, and spirit, meditation is something we *do* and mindfulness is something we *are*. Meditation is an intentional oasis in which you renew and replenish yourself. In meditation, you quiet your mind, body, and spirit in order to reconnect with yourself and your source. Meditation is an activity. Mindfulness is an intentional adjustment of attitude and focus.

Meditation supports and encourages mindfulness by training our wandering minds to be quietly aware and deliberately present. Because of its supportive nature, many of the practices included in *The Mindful Woman* are meditations. We do them to calm, center, and quiet ourselves and to diminish the tendency to become lost in thought. Such meditations strengthen the mindful muscles needed to develop the *habit* of mindful awareness.

Myth 2: Mindfulness Is Difficult and Time-Consuming

Because mindfulness is an attitude, we can move into it as easily and quickly as changing channels on the television. The only difficult parts of mindfulness are remembering to practice it and not judging ourselves when we forget, but simply choosing to move back into the moment and pay attention to what is going on right now.

Mindfulness actually saves time and energy because it eliminates the wear and tear that being sucked unconsciously into the past or future causes our psyches, souls, and selves. Although we can heal the past and plan for the future, we cannot change or control either, which often makes dwelling on them an exercise in frustration and impotence.

Differences Between Mindful and Automatic Living

All of us shift into automatic pilot occasionally. I know I do. But I didn't know how much I did until I decided it would be fun to take an inventory of my own mindful-/automatic-living quotient. During one particular day I curiously jotted down the times I noticed either mindful or mechanical actions or conversations. I was definitely wrong about the exercise being fun! Noticing how often I did or said things by rote—knowing that I probably missed about a million mindless examples—brought me up short and helped cement my commitment to living more mindfully one small step at a time. As a result of my little experiment, I realized that automatic living is essentially the opposite of mindfulness.

Because of the demands on our time, energy, and attention, many of us shift into overdrive in the morning and speed through the hours simply trying to get everything done that is expected of us or we expect of ourselves. At the end of such a day it's easy to wonder where the hours went, what we accomplished during them, and, more importantly, whether we feel it was a day wasted or well spent.

Sometimes just listing a few of the differences between mindful and automatic living gives us a clearer realization of the ratio of mindfulness to automatic living in our daily lives. The following examples barely scratch the surface of the differences between mindfulness and automation, but I imagine you can fill in the blanks with your own personal "favorites."

Mindful Living Is	Automatic Living Is
Conscious	Unconscious
Creative	Habitual
Calm	Restless
Simple	Complex
Purposeful	Chaotic
Responsible	Blaming
Mature	Immature
Grateful	Complaining
Empowered	Tyrannical
Openhearted	Fearful, protective
Relaxed	Rushed
Focused	Scattered

The antithesis of mindfulness is apparent in driving. My son once referred to driving as "downtime," but given the number of accidents and injuries happening every day, that's probably not the best way to think of it. Many of us do, however, use driving time to multitask and divide our time between the road, the phone, lunch, and scolding the kids, letting our minds wander the whole time. Police officers are now routinely asking drivers if they were on their cell phones at the time of an accident or infraction. Just the other day, I realized my inner autopilot had driven a few miles without me being aware of the road at all. Ironically, I was thinking about the topic of mindfulness so diligently that I became my own bad example.

Mindful living promotes peace and awareness, while a mind automatically overflowing with a million attention-grabbing thoughts and worries often creates anxiety, depression, and disappointment. When we're stretched to the limit and distracted by inner and outer demands, it's impossible to see anything clearly. Given the superhuman pace at which we often run, is it any wonder life seems to pass in a blur? On the other hand, mindfully moving through our days can bring a great sense of calm, balance, and joy. Even though I'm forever failing to remain mindful, simply holding an intention toward mindfulness and continuing to practice, practice, practice makes me feel good. Sir Winston Churchill's statement "Success consists of going from failure to failure without loss of enthusiasm" seems appropriate for the practice of mindfulness. We will fail to be mindful each moment—everyone does. But we can remain enthusiastic and glean benefits from our practice no matter how perfect or imperfect it is.

A Word About Women

Even though the practice of mindfulness is deeply rooted in ancient, monastic traditions, I believe women are uniquely suited to its practice because we are naturally blessed with qualities such as sensitivity and diffuse awareness. *Diffuse awareness* is the ability to comfortably perceive and understand many things at once. *Sensitivity* is having feelings about what is seen, understood, and experienced. Women are multi-focused, multifaceted, multitasking wonders. We are aware of and can pay attention to multiple things at once while also noting how we are feeling within the process. These are natural talents conducive to mindful living.

The upside of sensitivity and diffuse awareness is that nothing much slips by us; the downside is exactly the same thing. Nothing much slips by us. Although being acutely aware of and responsive to both subtle nuances and obvious occurrences is helpful in many areas of life—both child rearing and career-building spring to mind—such heightened sensitivity can also be overwhelming.

Sensitivity, Awareness, and Me

"I carry the weight of the world on my shoulders and feel overwhelmed and exhausted," a client lamented. I certainly could identify with her since I, too, felt overwhelmed for many years and made it worse by chastising myself for being a bad mom, wife, therapist, and whatever other hat I was wearing at the time. Yes, raising four kids, learning to live with two husbands—spectacularly *un*successfully in one case—running a household, cooking, creating a career and then another one on top of that, as well as doing the myriad everyday necessary stuff can be very exhausting. But I exacerbated the difficult feelings by neither understanding nor taking care of myself as well as I could have.

Noticing how often I seemed overwhelmed, a friend recommended I read Elaine Aron's 1998 book *The Highly Sensitive Person: How to Survive When the World Overwhelms You*. In the preface the author states, "Having a sensitive nervous system is normal, a basically neutral trait. You probably inherited it. It occurs in about 15 to 20 percent of the population" (xiii). Professor Aron goes on to explain that highly sensitive people's nervous systems are *physically* wired in ways that cause them to become overaroused and overstimulated more easily than most people.

Taking the self-test in the book showed beyond a shadow of a doubt that I was a highly sensitive person, an HSP. What an incredible relief to be labeled "normal" and to begin to let go of the gnawing fear that I was fundamentally defective or emotionally flawed beyond repair. Understanding that nervous system wiring—a physiological phenomenon—made me a sensitive person, not a wimp or, worse, a teeth-grinding bitch, continues to be an incredibly freeing insight.

Sound is one of my areas of greatest sensitivity. At the time I learned I was highly sensitive, my household was comprised of one husband, four teenagers, three dogs, a cat, and about a hundred friends of teenagers. As you can imagine, the noise level was off the charts. Even loving every kid, critter, and snorer didn't keep me from often feeling I was plugged into a high-voltage outlet ... with seemingly *no* outlet for my own feelings of failure, impatience, and bitchiness. Luckily, realizing how my nervous system and brain were wired gave me permission to begin setting boundaries that worked for me and weren't too restrictive for my family.

Because highly sensitive people gravitate to books like this, you may be an HSP. If so, it's especially important that you remain mindful of your sensitivity and, without judgment, take especially good care of yourself. Even if you think you don't have a sensitive bone in your body or a sensitive emotion in your psyche, it's still absolutely essential that you are mindful of your own needs and care for yourself as well as you do others. In our war-torn and often cruel world, I truly believe women are called to model kindness and well-being to the whole human race. And, of course, the best way to become such a model is to guard your own well-being as tenaciously and protectively as a loving mother would.

Feminine Qualities

Becoming mindful is an excellent avenue for self care and self-realization. In order to get the most out of mindfulness, you need to practice it in ways that are harmonious with your basic nature—a woman's way. The practices contained in *The Mindful Woman* concentrate on feminine strengths, qualities, and energies.

The following list of feminine qualities and energies is by no means complete. Rather, it is a sampling pointing out the intuitive, relational heart of femininity.

Feminine qualities include:

❋ *Diffuse awareness:* perceives and understands a wide range of stimuli simultaneously; expansive comprehension

❋ *Sensitive:* responsive to external and internal conditions or stimulation; susceptible to attitudes, feelings, or circumstances of self and others

❋ *Emotionally grounded:* steady, stable, well-balanced, able to bring all of her energy to exactly where she is in the moment

❋ *Intuitive:* holistic, accessing immediate perception rather than rational thinking; has a rich inner life

❋ *Relational:* interested in preserving and deepening relationships

❋ *Compassionate:* empathetic, warm, openhearted

❋ *Empowered:* with steeled softness, champions the weak and vulnerable and stands firm for what is right

❋ *Honoring of process:* is able to allow circumstances, ideas, and experiences to unfold

❋ *Gentle:* is able to live gently with herself and others

❋ *Forgiving:* realizes we are all imperfect and that nonforgiveness dams the natural flow of life force

✳ *Receptive:* is open to receive the new, different, and wondrous

✳ *Introspective:* is drawn to the spiritual and philosophical

✳ *Healing:* carries the ability to heal body, mind, and spirit through talent for listening deeply to her internal, inherent wisdom

Recognizing these feminine qualities as ones you possess or may aspire to possess can help you understand and respect the natural qualities you have and use them to lovingly and tolerantly guide you on your path to increased mindfulness.

Practice: Mindfully Inviting a Quality Through Breathing

Although the following breath practice is very simple, it is incredibly effective. By using your breath mindfully, you will invite a quality to live within you and, as a result, express through you naturally.

If one of the qualities listed above resonates with your heart, choose it for the practice. If not, please select a different quality you would like to embrace. For instance, a few days ago I felt frustrated and thwarted by circumstances beyond my control and, as a result, was impatient beyond belief. Because of the way I felt, choosing to breathe in patience was a no-brainer.

Unlike some of the more meditative practices, this one can be done anywhere. I did it while driving. The simple steps are:

1. Choose a quality you would like to embody.

2. Become aware of your breath.

3. As you inhale, imagine the quality being drawn deeply into your body and spirit. (It sometimes helps to give the quality a color. For me, patience was a muted salmon color.)

4. As you exhale, breathe out any resistance you may be holding toward anything—the practice, the quality, circumstances, whatever...

5. Consciously and deeply breathe in your chosen quality for at least seven full breaths, or more if doing so feels calming and centering.

As I was driving while consciously breathing in patience, I became acutely aware of the panorama of snow-covered Rocky Mountains ahead and felt as if the Divine Mother had gifted me with a beautiful example of stately patience. I like to imagine that beautiful vista as a reward for inviting a quality into myself that I was sorely lacking at the time and as an affirmation that such mindful efforts can bring beautiful results.

We use the introspection and inspiration frequently found within mindfulness practices as a way to know ourselves more intimately and, thereby, express ourselves in the world as we were created to do. Knowing yourself and being mindful of what your heart and soul long for and yearn to give is one of your highest callings. Philosopher Lao-tzu taught that "knowing others is wisdom, knowing yourself is enlightenment." All you are and can be is within. Your assignment is to pay attention and gently coax your unique authenticity into expression.

Insight is essential and can be exhilarating and very freeing. Gaining insight that I was a highly sensitive person was both. However, in order to create enduring life changes and be the best and happiest woman you can be, insight needs to be accompanied by both mindful awareness and positive action. The practices you'll be introduced to in this book are intended to strengthen that combination by using what I call the Insight ———> Awareness ———> Action progression.

Busy Women Can Be Mindful Too

Because women possess an innate ability to perceive an expanded range of feelings, thoughts, and experiences, we are adept at *consciously* handling several things at once. That doesn't mean you don't get frazzled and frustrated. It does mean you can feel even better and more productive by attentively, purposely, and nonjudgmentally staying in the present moment. Having qualities such as diffuse awareness and sensitivity means you already possess excellent tools for creating a more peaceful, loving, and mindful life. With awareness and intention, you can be mindful *within* your busyness—the caveat being that busyness needs to be comfortable and enjoyable, not a fear-based busyness. We'll explore both forms of busyness in various practices throughout the book.

Intention as Ally

Your thoughts and intentions announce your deepest wishes, desires, and goals to your subconscious mind, or inner sage, whose job it is to bring you more of what you project. It's great to have so willing a friend as long as your thoughts are positive and your intentions are set consciously. So often, however, they are neither. Many of our thoughts and intentions reflect deep-seated fears, unhealthy beliefs, and intolerances. For instance, if we fear we're not up to snuff in our job and think, "Good grief, how dense can I be?!" or "I'm never going to be able to learn all this!" sure enough, our brain, mind, and subconscious centers will obligingly provide what we ordered—feelings of inadequacy and stupidity. And, of course, such feelings make it hard for us to concentrate and keep us from learning as quickly and easily as we could if we were free from fear. Or, if we believe we're being treated unfairly, gnaw on feelings of being cheated, and long for revenge, once again the inner sage will obligingly present matching experiences and feelings.

Luckily, thoughts and intentions are equal-opportunity magnets. Actually, I choose to believe they are tipped ever so slightly toward the love and joy side of the equation. Yes, we can attract negatives, but our benevolent inner universe really seems to want to give us the good stuff more than it does the difficult. Consequently, thoughts of love, tolerance, acceptance, and general goodwill combined with conscious, positive intentions draw more good to us than we can even imagine. On the other hand, unhealthy, fear-based thoughts and intentions draw to us more of the same. Henry Ford was right when he said, "Whether we think we can or think we can't, we're right."

It's important to know that your subconscious mind is extremely literal and unable to discern between "true" and "false," "good" and "bad," or "positive" and "negative." What you say, believe, think, fear, and assume, the subconscious will do its darnedest to provide. The wonderful news is that knowing the nature of your inner sage gives you the understanding and ability to use the power of positive to mindfully set life-enhancing intentions that unerringly help you become a magnet for your desired results.

Intentions can be both expansive and minute. You can set far-reaching intentions, such as "My intention is to be a mindful woman," or intentions for the moment like, "My intention is to pay absolute attention to my next four breaths."

Expansive: *My intention is to become more loving.*

Minute: *I choose to respond (or stay silent) lovingly toward* _____ *right now.*

Expansive: *My intention is to be a healthy weight for my body type.*

Minute: *I am choosing to forgo this piece of candy right now.*

Intention is an invaluable ally on your journey toward increased mindfulness. One small step that can make a huge difference is to set an intention each morning before you are off and running. I might say, "Today I will be consistently kind." A favorite intention or affirmation if I'm worried about someone I love is "I place _____ in the arms of angels today and know that she or he is loved and protected."

Intentions are like personal angels who set our course and light the way to where we want to go and how we want to be in our lives, loves, and attitudes. Of course, because we're human beings, we'll fall short of our intentions time and again. When we do, it's important that we take an accepting, angelic approach and love ourselves back into alignment. Gentle correction is much more effective than criticism and judgment.

Why Choose Mindfulness?

Mindfulness is one of the most effective tools we can use to create more user-friendly brains. Have you ever noticed how easily your mind holds on to negative emotions and fixates on unhappy experiences? How much it loves to gnaw on hurtful scenarios and pick at the scabs on old wounds? I have. And I've felt really guilty and discouraged by it. So it is with great relief and joy that I welcome current brain research showing that our brain-mind complex is wired to emphasize negative experiences but can be taught to register positive experiences more deeply and quickly. Good-bye guilt, hello retraining.

Retraining the Brain

While there is an abundance of research on the brain-mind system, my main source for the following information is the online course Awakening Joy, created by James Baraz. Dr. Rick Hanson was a guest lecturer. Dr. Hanson spoke about research he and his partner, Dr. Rick Mendius, teach in their workshop Awakening Your Brain: Tools for Meditative Depth, Peacefulness, Happiness, and Equanimity. Dr. Hanson is a psychologist and Dr. Mendius a neurologist, and as such, they are well-equipped to provide information and insight on both the physical/medical and emotional/spiritual aspects of the brain and mind, which they see as one unified system.

Drs. Hanson and Mendius are in the process of writing a book with the working title *Buddha's Brain: The New Neuroscience and the Path of Awakening*. (Please go to www. WiseBrain.org for more information.)

Although the scope of *The Mindful Woman* does not permit a comprehensive exploration of Dr. Hanson and Dr. Mendius's research, with their permission, I have highlighted a simplified version of two points that are especially relevant to our a quest for mindfulness. I view the first as a good-news, bad-news scenario.

The Brain Emphasizes Negative Experiences

The "bad" news is that Mother Nature has wired our brains to register negative, fearful, and unpleasant experiences more deeply and vividly than it does positive, neutral, or pleasant ones. Why? Because she wants grandchildren. Therefore, we—her children—are programmed to survive above all else. Since avoiding negative experiences is more central to the survival of the species, they generally trump positive experiences. As an example, Dr. Hanson says, "A single bad event with a dog is more memorable than a thousand good experiences. The brain is like Velcro for negative experiences and Teflon for positive."

So where is the "good" news in this discovery? For me, this research answers my questions about why it is so easy to go into an emotional slump, be in a bad mood, obsess over slights, and any number of other "negative" behaviors and thought patterns that can seduce me away from my own happiness, peace of mind, and ability to love openheartedly and experience life with joyous and grateful abandon. Knowing my brain is wired for survival helps me understand that God/Mother Nature is simply trying to protect me by creating it that way.

And that leads to more good news. There is absolutely no reason to feel guilty or ashamed if we tilt in a negative direction now and then. As a psychotherapist, friend, and woman, it's been my experience that most women have a tendency to default to an at-fault position. If something goes wrong or someone is unhappy—including ourselves—we have a tendency to think, "What did I do wrong?" Simply knowing about our brains' propensity to accentuate the negative, we can breathe a collective sigh of relief and gently let ourselves off the blame/shame hook.

The best news of all is that we can retrain our brains to better absorb and savor positive experiences, beliefs, thoughts, and feelings.

Positive Experiences Are Best Registered in the Brain Through Conscious Attention

Sounds familiar, doesn't it? In fact, many of the avenues we will take on our journey toward making mindfulness a habit are strikingly similar to the ones Drs. Hanson and Mendius endorse in their workshop. Their research affirms that mindfulness offers us wonderful ways to befriend our brains and retrain our minds to attract and accept increased joy, peace, health, and relaxation.

It is a loving and practical choice to choose mindfulness because:

* Mindfulness adds value and meaning to life.

* Mindfulness helps you inhabit your life and, thereby, engage in and enjoy it more fully.

* Mindfulness calms your spirit, quiets your mind, and opens your heart.

* Mindfulness helps you feel you are on the right path, that you are *doing* life well and *being* who you are meant to be.

* Mindfulness brings out the best in you.

* Mindfulness relaxes your body.

✳ Mindfulness retrains your brain.

✳ Mindfulness enhances appreciation and gratitude.

✳ Mindfulness helps you break unhealthy habits.

✳ Mindfulness invites balance and harmony.

✳ Mindfulness enhances humor.

✳ Mindfulness minimizes scatteredness.

✳ Mindfulness helps you love yourself and others more deeply and freely.

Benefits of Mindfulness

Even though my dad described my infant-self as "an eel with insomnia," and I can still be fueled by uncomfortably distracted energy, I see undeniable signs that the moments of mindfulness I am able to sustain are creating a pattern within me for a quieter and more peaceful mind. The patter of regrets, what ifs, shame, and worry that used to plague me have, more often than not, been replaced by a softer attitude full of gratitude, contentment, and joy. My old habits of doing too much, resting too little, and putting myself last are transforming into healthy habits of self-care.

Among the most relaxing and grace-filled benefits I'm receiving from mindfulness are those of nonattachment, letting go, and lightening up, which are discussed in greater depth in part 3. As a matter of fact, after practicing mindfulness for a relatively short time, I was completely surprised when it gave me the courage and ability to let go of and develop compassionate detachment for situations that have weighed heavily on me for years. The ability to lovingly let go is a very pleasant and freeing surprise, I might add, and one that other mindful women have told me they enjoy also.

I credit a gentle, small-step approach to mindfulness practice with bringing more simplicity, love, freedom, and awareness into my mind, heart, and life.

Although we are not monks but busy women comfortably able to multitask much of the time, we have the wonderful ability to make our lives and hearts even happier and more joyous by learning to be increasingly mindful, in a feminine way.

Because you already lead a full and often complicated life, I've tried to design the practices in this book around a core of small, doable steps. The practices are simple and, hopefully, will entice you into regular, ever-expanding times of mindful presence. They issue an invitation to relax, revitalize, and reconnect with the essence of yourself and what makes life meaningful to you. Each practice was developed to help overcome distractions and strengthen your habit of mindfulness. They encourage you to be gentle with yourself as you move ever more surely toward enjoying the benefits to be gained from mindfulness. The practices can be as long or short as you like. Mainly, I hope you find them fun and effective. They are meant to be enjoyed.

Be gentle with yourself as you embark on or continue your mindfulness journey, and please remember that we all—even the masters among us—are *still* practicing.

In a Nutshell

✳ Feminine qualities such as sensitivity and diffuse awareness make women uniquely suited to the practice of mindfulness.

✳ Mindfulness is being nonjudgmentally aware of the present moment and fully engaged in the here and now.

✳ Four essential elements of mindfulness are paying attention, living in the moment, simplifying, and breathing.

✳ Although our brains are built to accentuate the negative, they can be retrained to better attract and absorb the positive.

✳ We intentionally choose to practice mindful living because the benefits from doing so make us happier, nicer, and more relaxed and fulfilled women.

A few mindful moments make a world of difference.

part two

the practices

chapter 2

cultivating compassionate awareness

Compassion for others begins with kindness to ourselves. —Pema Chödrön

For years, I have been teaching and writing that kindness toward ourselves is not only acceptable, but actually an incubator for increased compassion toward others. Nonetheless, the above quote from Pema Chödrön, an American Buddhist nun and teacher, still touches me. Her message that compassion for others is born from kindness to ourselves soothes the part of my psyche still valiantly trying to avoid the childhood admonition "Don't be so selfish!" Because I, and many women I talk with, seem to need at least intermittent reassurance that self-care is not synonymous with selfishness, the majority of the practices in this chapter are reminders to treat yourself as kindly and compassionately as you do others.

In order to treat yourself with consistent compassion and kindness, you need to be *aware* of what is happening in and around you. All insight and change begin with awareness. Without awareness, your choices are limited, and it's easy to get caught in the trap of repeating old habits and rehashing ancient hurts. However, being aware of what you are thinking and feeling enables you to intentionally, gently, and lovingly choose to change attitudes and actions that are no longer appropriate or desired.

Compassionate awareness is the cornerstone of mindfulness. With awareness, you become deeply attuned to yourself and increasingly appreciative of the people, opportunities, and, yes, the challenges life offers. Awareness is the first step toward both inner and outer change.

Beginning with Breath

The first thing you ever did for yourself was breathe. In order to enter into this life, you needed to take that first breath, no matter how scary or unfamiliar it felt to do so. And consciously focusing on your breath remains the epitome of self-care throughout your entire life. Breath is both starter and sustainer.

Have you ever noticed feeling tight and constricted when you are stressed, overwhelmed, or worried? Even during minor upsets, we tend to pull into ourselves like turtles retreating to the safety of their shells. In order to protect ourselves, we unconsciously get as small, compact, and hard as possible, which naturally leads to shallow, restricted breathing. The best thing you can do for yourself when you notice that you are barely breathing is to take a few deep, cleansing breaths.

We have a dogleg driveway that makes getting in and out of the garage pretty tricky. The other day I was cautiously backing my relatively new car out while concentrating hard on clearing both the garage door and the neighbor's fence behind me. When I had safely accomplished that feat, my husband chuckled and said, "Breathe, Susie." He was absolutely right. I had all but stopped breathing. His reminder made me laugh *and* take a deep breath.

It's ironic that our impulse to close down and constrict breathing during both mini and major crises is exactly the opposite of helpful. Shallow breathing depletes your resources, while breathing deeply oxygenates your brain, grounds you in your body, and maximizes your mental, emotional, and physical capabilities. Simply by reminding yourself to breathe, you can replace a detrimental, automatic reaction with a healthy one.

Practice...

✳ Before getting out of bed, intentionally focus on your breath.

✳ Take at least seven deep, conscious breaths.

✳ Thank your breath for faithfully sustaining you from the first moment of your life until now.

Throughout your day...

✳ Become aware of your breath and express gratitude for it.

Return to breath.

Stopping to Look, Listen, and Feel

Louise, a client of mine, was a sleepwalker who came to see me because she had awakened in the middle of the night about a block away from her home. As a psychotherapist, I was part of her support system while she waded through medical doctors and various medicines. Together we found a few exercises that cut her sleepwalking episodes in half. One was a simple awareness practice.

We started small. Before falling asleep, Louise affirmed, "I will wake up while I'm still in the house." Of course, she and her partner augmented the intentions and medications with practical tools like chairs in front of the doors. As she progressed, her affirmation of awareness became "I will wake up before I get out of bed." And she did. With practice and patience, Louise was ultimately able to stop all medication and sleep normally most of the time.

I couldn't help noticing how similar my own, and other clients', daytime rushing was to Louise's subconscious, nighttime meanderings. Without conscious commitment, awareness, and practice, it's easy to "sleeplive" our lives away. In order to awaken from the autopilot activity of sleepliving and savor life to the fullest, it's important to stop, look, listen, and feel. Because it's a shift in attitude and focus, the practice of *stop-look-listen-feel* can be done quickly at any time and in any place: while ironing, working at the computer, making love, cleaning the litter box, in class, dancing, cooking, driving...

Pausing to take note of what you're seeing, hearing, and feeling is an incredibly important touchstone for mindful living. A few sixty-second check-ins a day can make an amazing difference in how you feel and can also lay valuable groundwork for building mindful habits. As with all the practices, it's important to lovingly and gently accept and embrace what you discover.

$\mathcal{P}$ractice...

* Become aware when you have fallen into "sleep-living." (This may be the hardest part of the practice until you become accustomed to being aware of yourself.)

* Wake up to what you are seeing. What beauty is there to appreciate right now?

* Listen to the sounds around you. Identify one for which you are thankful.

* If a feeling is calling attention to itself, breathe deeply into the part of your body holding the feeling. Love the feeling, even if you would rather avoid or resist it.

$\mathcal{T}$hroughout your day...

* After each check-in, express—and *feel*, if you can—gratitude for the gifts of sight, hearing, and feeling.

With loving-kindness, pause to look, listen, and feel.

Paying Attention to Warning Signs

Although it's easy to forget to pay attention to ourselves, not doing so can be a potential killer. Marie, a young woman whom I love, is a single mother with two six-year-old girls, one biological and one adopted from overseas. Between a stressful full-time job, a deep love and commitment to parenting, the girls' child care, the expense and worry of work-related travel, and the kids' differing emotional needs, Marie fell into the habit of sticking self-care on the back burner.

Even after months of insomnia and several anxiety attacks, Marie continued to put her own needs after those of her children and her work. Luckily, the intense chest pains and inability to breathe that eventually sent her to the emergency room were not a heart attack. Actually, the ER visit was a blessing because, while there, Marie made the commitment to "make myself a priority!" And she has been true to that promise since then.

A former athlete, Marie has returned to running and other forms of exercise that promote her physical, mental, and emotional well-being. She no longer indulges in stress eating but consciously makes a choice for health before eating. After the first two weeks of her self-care commitment, Marie said, "The first week was tough, but I no longer want to make poor choices and already love me more!" She's become much more aware of her body's warning signs and, when she feels her heart flutter, takes an emotional and mental step back, breathes, and reminds herself of what's truly important to her. By listening to and lovingly responding to her body, the fluttering in her heart has never again escalated.

After congratulating Marie, I asked, "What's the thing that helps you the most in keeping your commitment to yourself?" Without hesitation, she replied, "Paying attention."

Practice...

✻ Take a few minutes to pay attention to the way your body feels.

✻ Without judgment, breathe deeply into any troublesome area.

✻ As you support the uncomfortable areas of your body with breath, ask them what they need from you. Responses are usually so subtle you will need to engage your intuition to discern what your body wants and needs. Even if it seems silly, trust your intuition, for it is the voice of inner knowing.

Throughout your day...

✻ Reaffirm your intention to pay attention to your body and take care of its needs.

You deserve to make yourself a priority.

Showering Yourself with Stars

Along with the brain-mind complex being wired to accentuate the negative, as we discussed in chapter 1, our self-assessments tend to be tilted toward the critical rather than the appreciative. I know I can gnaw on a comment I wish I hadn't made like a hungry buzzard ripping apart a carcass. And I can also feel like dead meat after a bout of such self-criticism. Because it bothers me so much, I usually do a reality check with people I fear I may have hurt. Many times, the people I've "wounded" don't even remember me doing or saying anything. Or, if they do and were upset, they are quick to understand and forgive.

We can learn a lot from those who are quick to understand and forgive and, as a result, commit to being generous and forgiving with ourselves. In fact, many of us probably need to take it a step further and make a commitment to concentrate on *appreciating* what we do and say, or refrain from doing and saying. We can break the habit of criticizing ourselves liberally while skimming over most of the loving, wise, and witty things we do and say. One lighthearted way to break the criticism habit is to accentuate and underscore the positive by giving ourselves actual gold stars for even the smallest accomplishment. For instance, if you are wrestling with depression or grief, you may gold-star yourself for getting out of bed that day. If the kids are driving you crazy, you deserve at least one gold star for *not* raising your voice, even though you feel like running from the house screaming, returning only to put them up for sale on craigslist.

Appreciation is the oil that lubricates life and keeps your wheels turning easily and freely. Without appreciation, your wheels will still spin, but they are apt to become rusted with resentment and exhaustion. Since there is great truth in the well-known statement "We teach people how to treat us," you can start teaching others to shower you with appreciation by showering yourself first.

Practice...

✳ Buy yourself gold star stickers—the bigger, the better.

✳ Have fun appreciating yourself and do so with over-the-top generosity.

✳ Each day, give yourself one or more gold stars for:
   ...something you said
   ...something you did
   ...something you wisely left unsaid or undone

Throughout your day...

✳ Give at least one other person a verbal (or actual) gold star.

You teach others to appreciate you by first appreciating yourself.

Taking Time-Outs

While many younger women may never have heard them, I was raised on a myriad of expressions like "Idle hands are the devil's workshop," "A man may work from sun to sun, but a woman's work is never done," and "It's good to stay as busy as a beaver." As a child, I must have taken the implied lessons in these platitudes to heart because, for most of my adult life, it was next to impossible to give myself permission to take a break during daylight hours. I was so brainwashed by those childhood sayings I often overlooked blatant signals that I had run out of steam and needed to take a break. As a result, I was often overtired, overworked, and overwhelmed, to say nothing about being royally ticked off at those around me who were mindful of their energy levels.

My dear friend, Bonnie, is a person who rests and, consequently, earned my ire early in our relationship. Her ability to rest eventually taught me incredibly valuable lessons about the art of taking time-outs. To this day, Bonnie is astutely aware of times when her energy dips too low and resolutely honors her need to rest. To boost her energy, she's been known to sit quietly with a cup of tea, adjourn a workshop we were cofacilitating to take a five-minute breather, or slip out of her own wedding reception to be restored by a few minutes of solitude in the sun. Before I could admit how absolutely horrible I was at paying attention to and honoring my own energy depletion, I projected onto Bonnie all the labels I was afraid would be pasted on me if I allowed myself to take rejuvenating time-outs. The fear of being thought selfish, rude, indulgent, or lazy kept me from being mindful of my own needs.

Although my brain has known for a long time that over-doing drains my reserves and rest is good for me, the awareness has only recently begun to sink into my gut. Of course there are times when we need to *choose* to tough it out and do what needs doing. Remembering to breathe deeply during tough-it-out times is immeasurably helpful, as is making sure you balance energy-draining times with restful and restorative interludes.

*P*ractice...

* In stressful situations, remind yourself to breathe and repeat, "I love myself ... I love myself."

* As soon as your energy dips below your comfort level, take a five- or ten-minute time-out. Breathe deeply and turn your face to the sun, if possible.

* If you cannot take a time-out, put your hand over your heart and sense or feel its beating.

*T*hroughout your day...

* Refresh yourself with at least three short, rejuvenating time-outs.

Have the courage to allow yourself time-outs.

Uncovering the Origin of Feeling

The most profound agents of creation are invisible. The two that spring to mind are God and thought. We enjoy the benefits and beauty of God's creations each moment and also reap the fruits of our thoughts throughout our entire lives. Whether our thoughts produce sweet or sour fruit is entirely up to us. It is a great kindness to fully embrace the idea that your thoughts are the origin of your feelings. Why? Because you have total control over your own thoughts and, consequently, have the power to choose those that bring you happiness and discard those that don't.

Imagine your mind as a garden and thoughts as the seeds you plant. Habitual negative, unhealthy, self-critical thoughts produce the weeds and thistles of depression, discontent, and anxiety in the garden of your mind. Luckily, the opposite is also true. Consistently planting positive, healthy, constructive thoughts will yield a crop of beautiful feelings, such as gratitude, love, and joy.

The hardest part of changing thought patterns is being aware of noxious thoughts before they sprout into full-blown negative feelings. Unhealthy thinking is a stubborn habit, often one we've built up over a lifetime. However, with patience and perseverance, any habit can be changed.

Uncovering and altering the origins of weedlike feelings is a process I've been practicing for decades, yet I still needed to do some pretty hefty pruning just yesterday. Due to family circumstances not of my own making, but nonetheless time-consuming and energy-consuming, I found myself feeling resentful, impatient, and definitely less than loving. In short, I was feeling bitchy and put-upon.

Thoughts such as "Good grief, yet another interruption in my writing process" and "When am I going to have the time for my *own* life and projects?" were generating feelings of poor me, poor little ol' beleaguered me.

Having uncovered the culprit thoughts, I changed them to positive, grateful ones, like "How lucky I am to have family to care for" and "I have all the time and energy I need to complete this book." It worked. In a few minutes, poor me became lucky me, and the feelings changed accordingly.

Practice...

❋ When a painful or angry feeling arises, notice it without judgment.

❋ Gently uncover the thought or thoughts creating the feeling.

❋ Even if it seems too simplistic to be helpful, *choose* to consciously change the negative thought to a positive one.

Throughout your day...

❋ Mindfully repeat the positive thought you have chosen each time the negative one sneaks back into your mind.

Thinking is the origin of feeling.

Recognizing Emotional Fallout

Whenever I begin writing a book, the imperial imp in charge of writers in early stages of projects seems to think that it would be great fun to have me act, feel, and express exactly the opposite of my current topic. When starting *The Courage to Be Yourself* (2001), I could have won the Appeaser of the Year award and, at the beginning of *Heart Centered Marriage* (1996), everything my husband did grated on my nerves. True to form, I was so scattered when first organizing *The Mindful Woman* that I began calling myself Dr. Ditzy, even though I know that is lousy self-talk. Although my lack of focus for everything except the book was a little amusing, it was also *really* frustrating. My fuse kept getting shorter and shorter until I completely lost my temper after the cat rode my treasured antique bamboo birdcage down the stairs for the umpteenth time. Wisely, cat, dog, and man all disappeared to safer rooms, and I was left steaming and storming (and picking up shards of bamboo) all by myself.

Recognizing that losing my temper was playing all sorts of havoc with my physical and emotional selves, I took a drive to assess the emotional fallout. Because I'm basically allergic to being enraged, I needed to reassure my churning stomach, constricted throat, and shamed inner child that everything was okay and *we* were okay, even though angry. As I was getting out of the car to get a Coke, I accidentally rammed my hand into the steering wheel, tearing my fingernail off past the quick. My initial response was unprintable until I noticed which finger was injured. The middle one, of course! Until the fingernail grew back, I had a humorous reminder that, for me, giving in to anger is not worth the emotional fallout.

In reality, thoughts create feelings and feelings cause both internal and external consequences. It's up to us to recognize which of our feelings are toxic and which are uplifting. With that awareness, we can mindfully and gently choose how to respond when feelings arise. Of course, we will not always choose well, but reassuring and loving ourselves usually helps free us from emotional fallout.

Practice...

✳ After giving in to a strong feeling, assess its effect on your body, mind, and emotions.

✳ If you are pleased with the aftereffects, give yourself a gold star.

✳ If you are not pleased, love yourself through your disappointment and set an intention about how to act differently next time around.

Throughout your day...

✳ Choose self-loving actions and responses.

You are a worthwhile and lovable woman even though you experience uncomfortable feelings.

Accepting Rather Than Rejecting

Have you ever noticed that you can change personalities to fit a mood or occasion as readily as you change clothes to suit the weather? One moment you can be an in-charge career woman, next a loving mom or friend, and then morph into the Wicked Witch of the West. If that is true for you, you're not crazy—you're simply moving between aspects of yourself as circumstances and feelings dictate. We all have several aspects, or subpersonalities, active within us at any given time. Some subpersonalities are healthier, happier, and more evolved than others. You can begin to enjoy all aspects of yourself by becoming aware of who's in charge in the moment, asking what they want and need, and then loving them to wholeness through acceptance.

Rose, a client, shared that during a meeting in which two people were monopolizing the time with inappropriate comments and jokes, she asked the part of herself feeling irritated and impatient, "What subpersonality are you?" In her mind's eye, Rose saw a spiky-haired cartoon character with crossed eyes and jangling nerves shooting out of her head. In answer to "What do you want?" the character snapped, "I want them to shut up!" (What is wanted is often a surface response, whereas what is needed is usually a core issue for subpersonalities.) When Rose asked, "What do you need?" the response was, "I just need you to understand how crazy all this jabbering is making me." Rose could easily oblige and, in the theater of her mind, nurtured her subpersonality by smoothing down her nerve-hairs, calming and holding her, and, most importantly, accepting her. It worked. And, as a result, Rose was able to make it through the rest of the meeting with a modicum of serenity.

We are always choosing between personalities. For instance, even if you are having an absolute meltdown, you would immediately switch to a helper personality if a child ran to you bleeding and crying. Becoming aware of your sub-personalities in order to consciously choose between them is incredibly empowering. Accepting and understanding your subpersonalities gives them an environment in which they can heal, transform, and express the positive qualities inherent within them.

Practice...

✳ Become acquainted with one subpersonality this week. Name her.

✳ Ask her what she wants and needs from you.

✳ To the best of your ability, give her what she needs.

Throughout your day...

✳ Give this subpersonality a pat on the back or a hug.

Each aspect of yourself is inherently valuable and worthwhile.

Living Gently with Yourself

What a wondrous kaleidoscope of contradictions, idiosyncrasies, and lovable qualities we women are. Many of the
paradoxes and quirks we display actually serve to make us
fun and interesting to be around. However, one contradic-
tion that can only breed low self-esteem, discouragement,
and often depression is treating others with gentleness while
heaping judgment on ourselves. You deserve and need your
own gentle support and thrive best when you are your own
trustworthy cheerleader.

Long ago I made up the motto "Live gently with yourself
and others" because I definitely needed to learn that lesson
myself. Because I continue to need reminders, my business
cards have sported the maxim since I was my only client and
my license plate reads LVGNTLY.

I believe one of our souls' major purposes is to know, love,
and express our authentic selves. To live the life and be the
person we were created to be. However, our true selves only
emerge when it's safe to do so. Self-condemnation, shame,
and guilt send your true nature into hiding. It's only in the
safety of gentle curiosity, encouragement, and self-love that
your soul can bloom as it was created to do. If I am right
about our souls' purpose, it's not only loving to treat ourselves gently, it's also a spiritual responsibility.

Treat yourself gently today, always, and in all ways. It is
the wise and soulful thing to do.

Practice...

✳ Set an intention to treat yourself gently and respectfully.

✳ If you become aware of treating yourself harshly, pause, take a centering breath or two, and thank yourself for noticing.

✳ Consciously return to treating yourself gently.

✳ It's okay to ask a friend or mate to help remind you to be gentle with yourself. My husband, Gene, says, "Is that gentle self-talk, Susie?" when I stray. (Although kind of annoying, it's helpful and usually makes me laugh.)

Throughout your day...

✳ Ask yourself, "Is this a gentle way to act ... respond ... talk to myself?" If the answer is no, choose a gentler way.

Gentleness invites your soul to soar.

Inviting Awareness Through Haiku

Creativity of all kinds focuses your mind, engages your imagination, and feeds your soul. Being creative can also facilitate understanding and encourage healing. Creativity is mindfulness in motion—intuitive, artistic motion. Creative moments and activities give you a boost and help you feel energized and good about yourself.

One creative endeavor I simply love is writing haiku poetry. Haiku is a type of poetry from the Japanese culture. It is simple and compact, and can include themes of nature, feelings, and experiences. Haiku has only three lines and rarely rhymes. The first line has five syllables, the second line seven syllables, and the third line five syllables. The fun and challenge of haiku is painting a mental picture in only three lines using a scant seventeen syllables.

Haiku offers a process of simplifying and distilling that invites new awareness and deeper understanding into our hearts and minds. For instance, when our family was experiencing a fissure over religious differences several years ago, I wrote the following haiku and sang it in front of a workshop full of people:

Wolves together stand
Howling soft and loud at light.
Singing family songs.

For reasons I've never fully been able to articulate, that little poem took much of the sting out of a trying period in my life.

One of the other things I appreciate about writing haiku is you can do it anywhere. During meetings or while waiting for a doctor's appointment, I often use haiku to soothe impatience and lighten my heart.

Please don't let the idea of writing a poem scare you. If you're like me, about one out of ten haiku will be keepers. So allow yourself to relax, enjoy the process, and maybe even learn to love it.

Practice...

✳ If you are feeling resistant to writing a haiku, encourage and support that aspect of yourself that is balking.

✳ Play at writing a haiku, even if part of you may be resisting.

5 syllables _____

7 syllables _____

5 syllables _____

Throughout your day...

✳ Do something creative one or more times today. (It doesn't have to be haiku.)

**Becoming aware,
Live gently with yourself by
Paying attention.**

chapter 3

being at home
in the moment

*If we could see the miracle of a single flower
clearly, our whole life would change.* —Buddha

I vividly remember a time when I completely understood what the Buddha meant about seeing the miracle of single flower being life changing. My husband, Gene, and I had a trans-Pacific-ocean courtship. To help bridge the miles, he once sent me red roses. After my sons were asleep, I took the time to luxuriate in every aspect of the fullest rose, exploring its textures, colors, and the varying shapes of petals, stem, and stamen. To my surprise, tears of joy began to slip from my eyes, and I felt enveloped in love and connected to both the man who sent the roses and their creator as well.

Although my rapt attention to the flower was the act of a young woman wildly in love, the experience of it has become an enduring touchstone reminding me of the power and joy a few mindful moments can bring. Thirtysome years later, I clearly remember that particular rose and can revisit the profound sense of wonder and awe I experienced while focusing on it.

Obviously not all our moments are coming up roses. In fact, many of them are extremely painful and sad. No matter what it contains, the moment is still our home. As Vietnamese monk Thich Nhat Hanh says, "The present moment is where life can be found, and if you don't arrive there, you miss your appointment with life." As well as highlighting happy moments, the practice of mindfulness can help us find a glimmer of understanding, gratitude, awe, and hope in even the most difficult times.

By being mindfully at home in the moment, we keep our appointment with life.

Taming the Monkey Mind

While living in Hawaii, we visited a restaurant that boasted a Monkey Bar. Behind the bartender and rows of liquor bottles was a glass partition shielding patrons from the smell and splatters of the countless monkeys living there. Relentless chatter, unceasing motion, and restless picking at each other made me acutely uncomfortable. Not only did I feel sorry for the monkeys, but their actions stirred up something in me that made it impossible to relax and enjoy dinner.

Talking with a client a few days later, the answer to my upset popped out of my mouth unbidden. While discussing her feelings of anxiety, I said, "It sounds like your mind was chattering away at you as chaotically as the monkeys at the Pearl City Monkey Bar do." Bingo! A big reason I was disturbed by those wild little monkeys was they reminded me of my own restless and overactive mind chatter.

Having seen the Monkey Bar inhabitants up close, it makes total sense that the term "monkey mind" has become a modern colloquialism, especially within contemplative communities. However, I believe monkey mind doesn't apply only to those who try to meditate but is a reflection of the scattered nature of our culture as a whole.

In order to stop the stress of thinking and doing too much at once, it's important to notice when thoughts or actions begin to disrupt each other and you feel frazzled. The very beginning of frazzledness is the time to gently and lovingly choose to simplify. If your mind is overfull and flighty, you can easily get sucked into a whirling black hole of responsibility, obligation, and stress. Overwhelmed by such uncomfortable feelings, it's easy to miss any peace and beauty that may be available in the current moment.

Mindfulness helps you be fully present to your authentic self and live your life with acute awareness and an open heart. A wonderful way to open your heart more fully is to be patient and kind to yourself, even if your monkey mind seems incorrigible. Maintaining a patient attitude is easier when we remember that long-term mindfulness practitioners remain adamant that taming the monkey mind is never a fait accompli but an ongoing, lifelong learning process.

Practice...

✳ Simply notice when your mind is leaping about distractedly and chattering incessantly.

✳ Focus on a single thought and repeat it yourself several times.

✳ If your mind wanders, gently return your attention to the single thought.

✳ No matter how you feel about the result of your efforts, congratulate yourself for practicing.

Throughout your day...

✳ Give yourself a mental gold star each time you notice and refocus mind chatter.

Give yourself the gift of encouragement.

Choosing a Positive Attitude

I was overwhelmingly touched by the attitude of a young couple I met while volunteering as a hospice chaplain. I visited their home because Jim, the husband, was in the last stages of cancer, and they wanted to talk about his eventual memorial service. Because they were a young couple with kids, I was anticipating a somber, grief-stricken atmosphere. I was wrong. Jim's wife, Morgan, greeted me at the door with a smile and said, "Hi, come on in. The house is kinda chaotic 'cause the kids are at the tail end of a sleepover and on a sugar high." With the exception of the gaunt young man lying on a hospital bed in the living room, the energy of both house and inhabitants was exactly what you'd expect from one brimming with sleep-deprived, sugar-stimulated kids—loud, boisterous, and happy.

Over the course of the next few weeks, Jim and Morgan taught me many lessons about appreciating each moment and looking on the bright side of things. Of course, they had their down times and she had fears about the loneliness of a life without Jim and how she could be both mom and dad to the kids. But underneath every joy and each heartache was an incredible stability and a belief that life was good. After several weeks, I asked how they maintained such a positive attitude. Both credited their parents for teaching them to accentuate the positive and look for the good, happy, and beautiful in everything. "It's just become second nature," Jim explained a few days before he died.

Although many of us probably didn't get such a thorough education in the value of a positive attitude, we *can* teach ourselves. Simply by making a decision to look for the good, happy, and beautiful in all things and all people, you will have completed the first and most important step in learning to accentuate the positive. As with any new knowledge, it's best to start with the fundamentals and not overwhelm yourself by expecting to learn everything perfectly by tomorrow. Start slowly, and gently keep on keeping on.

Practice...

∗ Set an intention to be more positive and look for the good, happy, and beautiful within all experiences and people (including yourself).

∗ Jot your intention down in a place where you'll see it often. Visual reminders enhance intention.

∗ Before going to sleep, remind yourself of the positive things, thoughts, and feelings you experienced throughout the day.

Throughout your day...

∗ Each hour, look for the good, happy, or beautiful in one thing, person, experience, or bit of nature.

A positive attitude lightens your heart.

Enjoying Everyday Beauty

The universe is extremely generous. Beauty abounds in the most surprising locales and within even the most soul-searing experiences. We simply need to look for beauty and take the time to appreciate and digest what we see. I agree with Margaret Wolfe Hungerford's quote "Beauty is in the eye of the beholder" and would add that beauty is also in the beholder's ability to *see*.

The other night I was gifted with an unexpected beauty when I took our little dog, Lily, out to her piddle place, a fenced-in area beside the house. It is hidden from the road and "landscaped" meagerly with rocks. Its sole decoration is the garbage can. Expecting the same old bedtime routine, I was blessed by beauty instead. The streetlight, which goes on and off sporadically, was backlighting the brand-new, fuzzy catkins on our neighbors' aspen tree. They looked as if they were encased in sparkling ice, shimmering and dancing in the early spring breeze. An awed "Ahhhhhh" escaped as I exhaled. While Lily did what she was supposed to do, I turned off our light, etched the beauty of the lighted catkins in my mind's eye, and whispered a prayer of gratitude for a lovely surprise in such an everyday place and action.

While the beauty of the illuminated aspen would have been hard to ignore, I easily could have done just that before making the promise to myself to lead a more mindful, appreciative, and in-the-moment life.

In order to enjoy everyday beauty, you need a desire to see it and the willingness to open your heart to it. It helps when you go about your day *expecting* to be blessed by beauty everywhere you look and turn. Expecting and paying attention to the beauty of the moment will draw to you loveliness beyond imagination. Appreciating and reveling in beauty can soothe your soul, relax your body, and immerse you in gratitude.

Practice...

＊ Expect to find beauty in the strangest places.

＊ Allow yourself to look for beauty everywhere.

＊ Enjoy and appreciate the beauty you notice.

＊ Allow yourself to really *see* a single aspect of your own beauty.

Throughout your day...

＊ Notice and appreciate at least one of Mother Nature's everyday beauties.

**Beauty is in the eye of beholder
expecting to see it.**

Surrounding with Space

Just for fun, where did your eyes first go when looking at this page? If it was to the sentence encircled in white space, you already know the point of this practice.

Space enhances that which it surrounds.

Artists, musicians, parents, decorators, public speakers, animal trainers, florists, and actors are among the many people who know the value of accentuating their art with silence and space. Any of you who have framed (or even admired) a photograph or written an invitation in calligraphy know about calling attention to the focal point by surrounding it with space. Art galleries leave space between paintings to allow viewers to concentrate on one piece at a time. And musicians, including our church choir director, Kamilla Macar, say it is the interplay between sound and silence that helps make music meaningful.

Similarly, body and soul are soothed when activity is framed by pauses.

If our activities are lined up endlessly, we must race through them like an athlete running the hurdles in a track-and-field competition. Jump, sprint, jump, sprint, jump ... In contrast, having time and space—even the smallest amount, as long as it is allotted consciously—around activities invites us to savor, absorb, and actually *experience* them. Pauses allow your spirit to catch up with your body.

While there are a few women who seem to thrive in overdrive, the majority of us run the risk of depleting our immune systems, draining our emotional reserves, and fraying our nerves if we run too fast for too long.

Take a look at your calendar, organizer, or PDA. Can you see white space? If not, how might you begin to surround your activities with space? Where would you like to pause?

Practice...

* *Under*schedule one day this week. If that is too difficult, consciously underschedule one hour in the next two days.

* Take pleasure in the white space you create.

Throughout your day...

* Surround several activities with mini spaces. For instance, pause quietly for a few moments after each phone conversation, or take a few minutes after lunch to simply *be*.

Space enhances that which it surrounds.

Feeding Body and Soul

We all know food is a necessary fuel for keeping us alive, alert, and healthy. From experience, many of us also know that the idea of food carries a lot of baggage. The "Hollywoodizing" of body norms, underlying beliefs about our own weight and attractiveness, and how much comfort we get from eating can combine to create a love/hate relationship with food. Too much food ... guilt. Too little food ... guilt. The wrong kind of food results in yummy taste laced with guilt and a lack of wellness. Good food results in often needing to change our taste preferences and worry over expense. I could go on and on, and I imagine you could also.

I'm told that mindfulness can bring you into a whole new relationship with food and eating, which is good news to me because I love to eat. Eating is a complete pleasure for me. I shake my head in wonder—and reach for chocolate—when someone says they can take it or leave it and really eat only to stay alive. Say what?! As you can imagine, weight has been an ongoing issue for me. With effort, exercise, and lots of self-control—not a virtue at which I am adept—I can usually keep myself within shouting distance of an appropriate weight. However, due to some injuries that curtailed exercise for quite a while, combined with the comfort factor of food, I am nowhere near appropriate right now.

I have, however, given up guilt and am working on mindful eating to help change old habits, enjoy different foods, and eat more healthily. Want to join me? Even though I've been thinking, writing, and dreaming about mindfulness for months, I haven't been eating with it until a few short days ago. No, my weight hasn't changed yet. No, I don't feel more energized or bouncy yet. What has changed, though, is that I am much more aware of my body and how it responds to what I feed it.

The following practice is what I'm doing to encourage myself to eat mindfully. You will undoubtedly have your own way of doing it. Please listen to the information your unique body gives you and follow its wisdom.

Practice...

✳ Consciously *choose* what you eat.

✳ Sit down to eat (not in a car, unless it's stopped).

✳ Pay attention to each bite. Chew slowly.

✳ Only eat. Or accompany eating only with conversation.

✳ Feel gratitude for the food you eat.

✳ Notice how the food you eat affects your body.

Throughout your day...

✳ Congratulate yourself for each mindful choice you make.

Mindfully eaten food is a friend to both body and soul.

Blessings of Breathing

Breathing is the best medicine. Not only does it keep us alive, it can also interrupt negative thought patterns, bring new vitality to needy body parts, encourage deep sleep, calm quaking nerves, and infuse the brain with energy and power, to name but a few of its benefits.

Blessing with breath is as simple as it is effective:

* *Paying attention to breath.* Become aware of your breath. Notice the breath entering and leaving your nostrils.

* *Deepening breath.* Gently deepen your breath. Sense the expansion of your body on the in breath, and enjoy the relaxation of the out breath.

* *Directing breath to bestow blessings.* You can direct your breath to anyone or anything. If a friend is having a difficult time, bless them as you breathe out. Something as simple as "Bless you" or "Peace to your heart" is great. Words are not even necessary. Consciously intending to bless another with breath is good enough.

I find it comforting to bless myself with breath if I'm nervous, worried, grieving, or upset in any way. Paying attention to my breath, I might ask that God's blessings flow into me as I inhale and that anything I need to let go of flows out as I exhale. Inhaling the positive and loving and then exhaling the negative and detrimental usually has a calming influence on me.

If someone gets under my skin and I allow irritation and negative thoughts to chafe my psyche, I can often interrupt such self-sabotaging behavior by exhaling a blessing toward the person with whom I am annoyed. Choosing to bless rather than holding onto irritation and annoyance is a blessing in itself. Sending blessings calms the mind, soothes the heart, and helps break the habit of letting irritations or annoyances obscure our joy.

Practice...

* Use a few breaths each morning to consciously invite blessings into your body, mind, and emotions.

* When you think of someone you love, send them two or three breath blessings.

* If you become upset with someone, breathe blessings toward them.

Throughout your day...

* Breathe love and acceptance into yourself and breathe out goodwill to others.

Breath is an original blessing.

Keeping Hope Afloat

Hope is an inside job. Although poet Alexander Pope said, "Hope springs eternal in the human breast," hope springs faster and more consistently when we consciously encourage and consistently practice keeping hope afloat in our hearts and souls. In order to keep hope alive, it's extremely important that we monitor what we allow ourselves to see, hear, and feel, especially in regards to the media. Because our subconscious minds accept as real not only our personal experiences but also those we watch or imagine vividly, it's up to us to choose mindfully and wisely what we watch and read.

Because images imprint deeply, the disturbing pictures and commentary favored by the media can act as an emotional acid, etching the pain and suffering we witness into our own psyches. Such images can pull the plug on our reserves of hope. Limiting your exposure to sensationalism of all kinds is wise. Allow yourself to be as *in*formed as you feel the need to be but not *de*formed by overexposure and overstimulation.

Hope is so important because it's the proverbial light at the end of any dark tunnel encountered. Hope is the ballast that keeps you moving forward and helps you continue to believe in beauty, love, and survival, even when your personal waters are incredibly rough. With hope, it's easier to keep your head above water while navigating stormy seas. Hope makes normal, everyday life much brighter and more joyous.

My friend Anne provides a great example of how to nurture hope in hard times. During the inevitable dark times of aggressive breast cancer treatments, she consciously courted hope. Allowing people to help (not a familiar feat for her) and using Julian of Norwich's famous prayer "All shall be well, and all shall be well, and all manner of things shall be well" as her mantra were two of her most important hope boosters. Anne also intentionally chose to be a student of cancer rather than its victim and, as such, kept asking herself invaluable questions, like "What lesson am I learning here?" and "What is cancer trying to tell me?" After the completion of surgery and treatment, Anne stood in front of her church family and, with grace and gratitude, shared her journey with us. Hers were about the only dry eyes in the congregation.

Practice...

✳ Promise yourself to keep hope afloat in your heart and soul.

✳ If you find yourself in the dark, search out a speck, flash, or ray of light right here, right now.

✳ Intentionally look on the bright side.

Throughout your day...

✳ Three times a day, take a moment to find a spark of hope in nature, your own life, your home, or the life of a friend or loved one.

Hope is contagious. Please spread it.

Rebelling with Radical Wisdom

In our fast-paced, future-obsessed society, aspiring to fully inhabit each moment is radically wise and, actually, a subtle form of rebellion against the less-than-mindful status quo.

I don't know about you, but as a dedicated "nice girl," a bit of rebellion appeals to me. Mindfulness as rebellion ... I like it! If you and I start a mindfulness revolution within our own lives, who knows where it might lead? While living an increasingly mindful life, could we, personally or globally, condone war? Could we allow children to starve? Could we remain quiet in the face of injustice? Could we take those we love for granted? Actively engaged in the radical wisdom of mindfully living in the present moment, could we treat *ourselves* unkindly? I don't think so.

We women are wonderfully powerful and wise, plus more influential than we dare imagine. Which, of course, means that *you* are powerfully wise and influential. As with all worthwhile endeavors, being aware of and accepting your own radical wisdom begins internally. Paying attention to the wisdom, grace, and courage you express in the moment provides a treasure trove of insight into your own incredible qualities and gives you the audacity to rebel in conscious, peaceful ways.

With mindfulness, even difficult times can be incredibly revealing and enlightening. They help you know yourself better, appreciate your strength and wisdom more deeply, and increase your capacity for compassion.

The current moment is your home, your solace, the only place and time where you can find balance, happiness, and empowerment. Settling into each moment as it really is, not as you wish it were, allows you to appreciate your life in all its sadness and glory.

Practice...

* Sit quietly for a few breaths and simply pay attention to the moment, no matter what it holds or how it feels.

* Jot down three ways in which you are wise right now. (It isn't necessary to be *acting* on the wisdom.)

* At least once a day, ask for guidance in using your wisdom. Breathe in guidance; breathe out resistance to your own power and influence.

Throughout your day...

* Several times, breathe out the affirmation, "My wisdom blesses me and the world." You don't have to believe the statement. Simply make a commitment to repeating it with as much feeling as possible, and miracles can happen.

**Radical wisdom
Blooms when powerful women
Practice mindfulness.**

chapter 4

savoring the qualities of a quiet mind

We need to be quiet. We need to be happy. We need to be still. God's holy peace is all around me. When I am still, it is reflected within me. —Hugh Prather

I've chuckled with friends who, like me, are trying to live mindfully, that we might make better progress if we started a new 12-step program called SAA: Stimulation Addicts Anonymous. There certainly have been times in my life when I could have benefited from meeting with a supportive group and admitting my addiction to the emotional roller coaster of drama, trauma, and constant activity. As a young woman, I was lucky enough to have my own personal SAA sponsor in the form of Annabelle Woodard, my spiritual mother and mentor. Annabelle gently showed me I was a stimulation junkie. "Your mind is always in turmoil, Sue, and your life is like a roller coaster, soaring to very high highs and crashing to equally low lows." I, of course, dramatically denied it at the time. She, of course, was right.

Although I now see myself as a recovering drama queen, it still takes consistent awareness to avoid being sucked into the stimulation vortex to which our society as a whole seems addicted. For me, and many other stimulation addicts, mindfulness is a wonderful form of rehab. Being mindful helps free us from the habitual firestorms of mental and emotional chaos, excessive busyness, and the debilitating habits of anxiety, worry, and guilt.

In this chapter, I have chosen to highlight a few of the qualities inherent in a quiet mind. The qualities we'll be working with are clarity, equanimity, choice, tolerance, optimism, wisdom, awe, receptivity, and spaciousness. The practice of these qualities can help you be happy and still and, hopefully, even reflect the peace of God to our beleaguered but nonetheless beautiful world and her inhabitants.

Seeing with Clarity

Feelings of confusion, ambiguity, and murkiness are incredibly uncomfortable. In the throes of such feelings, we want to move ahead but don't have a clue as to which direction to turn. We long for the relief of making a good decision but can't decide which is the right one. We want to make a choice, but each has both pros and cons, and we simply can't bring ourselves to say, "That's the one!"

If this sounds familiar, what can you do? Nothing … *Nothing!?* Yep, nothing. Many years ago, Elisabeth Kübler-Ross MD, the eminent psychiatrist who brought the subjects of death, dying, and grief out in the open, introduced me to a little book by Grace Cooke entitled *The Quiet Mind* (1972), saying it was the only thing that helped her quiet her own mind. If Elisabeth, a dynamo of constant energy, was helped by this book, I had to have it. *The Quiet Mind* is a collection of short paragraphs by the spiritual teacher White Eagle. My favorite passage—one I often turn to when opening the book at random—is "If you do not know what to do, do nothing." White Eagle goes on to say we need to still our minds and not act from confusion. He believes that clarity and right action can best surface from the depths of a quiet, serene mind. I have found this to be true.

Of course, the mindful approach to doing nothing when feeling unclear is not really doing nothing. To gain clarity, you breathe. You wait. You ask for clarity. You sit quietly and consciously invite your mind to settle. You visualize clarity. You accept yourself just as you are right in this murky moment. You trust that clarity will come. And you turn your awareness to the ebb and flow of the current moment. Returning to the here and now interrupts the mental wheel spinning that inevitably accompanies confusion and doubt.

Practice...

* Without judgment, notice when you feel unclear or confused and resist the impulse to act from uncertainty.

* Sit quietly with your eyes closed for a few minutes and concentrate as fully as possible on the inflow and outgo of your completely reliable breath.

* For the next several breaths (at least seven, please), silently affirm, "I know that I know," as you inhale and say, "Thank you," as you exhale.

Throughout your day...

* Sing snatches of uplifting songs, such as Johnny Nash's oldie about seeing clearly now that the rain is gone.

* Repeat "I know that I know" or "I trust that I know" whenever you remember to or when you begin to feel anxious.

You *do* know.

Experiencing Equanimity

When you think of the word "equanimity," you may think of things like mental or emotional composure and stability in all circumstances, steadiness of mind under stress or tension, or calmness and equilibrium. A few of my own definitions are letting go of how we think things "should" be, radical acceptance, and not getting our knickers in too tight a knot over anything, especially that which we can't control.

Being a lover of words, the word "equanimity," itself, appeals to me. "Equanimity" has a wonderful flowing sound that brings to mind an unhurried mountain stream leisurely making its way toward reunion with its source. Nothing deters or disturbs such a stream. Faced with obstacles, it does not resist or give up resentfully but, rather, resolutely and peacefully finds a way to continue its journey.

Many women, myself included, do not come into this life as naturally even-tempered, accepting, free-flowing people able to remain calm and peaceful no matter what the circumstances. Some of us feel more like storm-tossed seas than tranquil streams. Lori, my dental hygienist, was a turbulent sea. "I used to lock and load on the differences between myself and others and allow that to irritate and nag at me and separate me from them," she explained. "But I'm a totally different person now. Even though there's been no change in my circumstances, there's been a huge change in my attitudes and feelings. And my blood pressure's a lot lower."

How did Lori make the transformation? By practicing meditation and mindfulness. Although Lori meditates at least forty minutes a day and sometimes as long as three hours at a time, she stresses that consistency is more important than time. I hope she's right, because most of us will not meditate for hours on end and *all* of us will lapse in and out of mindfulness regularly. Fortunately, we can always invite equanimity back into our lives and selves by returning to mindfulness and consistently gifting ourselves with quiet times.

Practice...

✳ Accept yourself just as you are right now, whether wild and stormy or calm and peaceful.

✳ Set the intention to quiet your mind and move toward equanimity.

✳ With your eyes lightly closed, imagine your breath as gentle undulations of cool, tranquil water. Allow yourself to be soothed by the soft, sweet movement.

Throughout your day...

✳ Consciously ride the gentle waves of your breath for a few moments at least two or three times. This may also be a good way to lull yourself to sleep.

Breathe yourself calm and composed.

Making the Best Choice

Choice is freedom. As with most freedoms, choice carries tremendous responsibility. We want to make choices that resonate with our heart's desires and keep us going in the right direction. In addition, as women, we are usually very cognizant of making choices that are also good for those we love.

Each day you have many opportunities to state a preference, mull over options, and choose between alternatives. A majority of the time choices are simple. Cereal or eggs? Jeans or a skirt? Other choices are life altering. Have children or not? This job or that one? Surgery, chemotherapy, or holistic treatment?

Simple choices are easy and often made by rote. Difficult choices, however, are best made from the clarity of a quiet mind.

After being diagnosed with cancer, my dear friend Catherine was faced with a barrage of choices. Naturally, she wanted to make those that gave her the best chance of recovery and also do what brought a modicum of solace to her husband, daughters, and large extended family. Although an exceptionally clearheaded and independent woman, Catherine understandably experienced some confusion while sorting and culling her options, managing her own feelings, and being considerate of others' feelings as well.

In answer to my query about how she had decided what treatments to pursue, Catherine answered, "Finally, I simply had to tell everyone—family and doctors included—to leave me alone for a while. I needed solitude to uncover what I really thought and felt." She returned from a silent weekend retreat "knowing in my heart what I needed to do."

Each time I visited Catherine during and after treatments, we followed a little ritual. First I asked her how her body was and she gave me as much of an update as she wanted to share. Next I asked how her heart was. Without fail, her answer was "My heart is good. My heart is always good." Even though the outcome was not the one for which we hoped and prayed, Catherine's peace of mind never faltered, partly, I'm sure, because she had quieted her mind enough to follow her heart.

Practice...

✳ When faced with serious decisions, be very mindful of the scared, angry, or hurt part of yourself and nurture her in ways that feel good. Remember to be loving rather than judgmental toward yourself.

✳ Take time for solitude. Breathe in serenity and peace. Breathe out anxiety and confusion.

✳ Gently, but deeply, breathe into your heart, asking it to help you make the right decision.

Throughout your day...

✳ Bring your awareness to your heart and breathe peace, calm, and quiet into it.

**A quiet mind allows you to
choose from your heart.**

Upping Tolerance Levels

We will be exploring two kinds of tolerance in this practice: tolerance for living beings and tolerance for circumstances. Tolerance for living beings, ourselves included, consists of having an attitude of acceptance and fairness coupled with genuine respect. Tolerance for circumstances is our ability to tolerate unfavorable conditions that can run the gamut from slightly irritating to disastrous.

So what does a quiet mind have to do with tolerance levels? Quite a bit. If your mind is in flea-on-a-hot-griddle mode, it will automatically revert to habitual beliefs, feelings, and actions in order to hurry on to the next thing. A quiet mind, on the other hand, is aware of alternatives and has the freedom to choose among them. A small example happened to me this morning. I was driving to my grandson's baseball game and a young man in a truck kept riding my bumper. Before practicing mindfulness, tailgating was one of my favorite intolerable annoyances. Well, truth be told, I was pretty annoyed this morning for a few minutes also, *until* I remembered to quiet my mind.

A quiet mind can return to the moment and wake us up to what is really happening now. Is the driver kissing my tailpipe *really* making my drive intolerable? No. Is he a selfish, thoughtless, chauvinist clod who shouldn't be allowed on the road? Probably not. By now I was smiling and gently chiding myself about how easily I regressed to old thoughts and how quickly I became upset as a result of them.

It felt so good to remember the situation could be seen and experienced differently. For fun, I created a new story, one in which the villainous clod became a dedicated husband

and father who was rushing to be with his family for some important reason. Given my new tolerance of Mr. Tailgater, I actually felt like sending him a little blessing rather than the original gesture I'd wanted to make.

A quiet mind is a peaceful mind. From the steady calm of a quiet mind, you have the ability to remember that tolerance is best found in the here and now of the current moment.

Practice...

✳ When you feel intolerant or upset, bring your attention to the current moment. Feel your feet on the floor and be aware of your breath.

✳ If you notice a negative mind-movie running in your head, have a little fun by changing it to a positive drama or comedy.

✳ Send a brief blessing to sources of irritation or intolerance.

Throughout your day...

✳ Notice your feet and the surface upon which they rest.

Tolerance is a kissin' cousin of compassion.

Cultivating Cockeyed Optimism

Most of us know at least a little bit about the black holes wandering around our galaxy. We know, for instance, that a black hole will voraciously gobble up any star, planet, or cosmic debris in its path. Pessimism is a lot like a personal black hole. Left unchecked, pessimism darkens your attitude, swallows your hope, and effectively squelches any enthusiasm you might otherwise feel for circumstances, experiences, and other people.

Studies show optimists live longer, heal faster, have more friends, and enjoy life more than pessimists. Given such good reasons to cultivate optimism, why do we occasionally find ourselves slumping through our days like Eeyore lamenting the inadequacies of his tail? One reason is that pessimism is easier than optimism. Simply reading newspapers, watching the news, and paying attention to the pessimistic people around us can be enough to suck us into the black hole of gloom and doom.

In reality, the least productive thing you can do, both personally and globally, is to allow your days to be devoured by black-hole pessimism. Concentrating on the "ain't it awfuls" permits pessimism to become your psyche's default setting. Acute pessimism also stops you from effecting a positive outcome to problems that need solving.

On the other hand, because optimists look on the bright side of events and conditions and expect the most favorable outcome in all situations, they have the energy and enthusiasm to do their part in making sure tomorrow will be better than today. Optimism fuels forward movement and hope. Cultivating optimism gives you the ability to be happier and healthier in the present while also shaping a more positive future for yourself and your loved ones. Optimists get things done. Fabulous work, beautiful babies, cures for disease, and great relationships, as well as most other worthwhile endeavors, are usually fueled by cockeyed optimism. An attitude of "I think I can ... I think I can ..." proves true more often than not.

*P*ractice...

✳ Gently, but with great commitment, change pessimistic thoughts to optimistic ones. (Believing the thoughts is not necessary for this practice to work.)

✳ As much as possible, associate with upbeat people.

*T*hroughout your day...

✳ Notice at least two or three examples of optimism. A small ant moving a large crumb, a toddler getting up from a fall to try walking again, a plant growing out of a rock crevice, an old couple holding hands...

**An optimist isn't always happy,
but she thinks she will be soon.**

Tuning In to Wisdom

Wisdom is not book learning but, rather, a quality or state of *knowing* what is true or right coupled with the judgment to discern constructive action. Wisdom is the insight and intuition contained in the proverbial still, small voice that only a quiet mind can hear and know. I love the way Nat Carter, a Unity minister, describes the voice within: "The still, small voice within us is polite. It waits for space to be heard, not raising its volume or interrupting to get our attention." Darn! There are definitely times when I'd prefer my inner wisdom to cut through all the mind chatter, speak in a loud, large voice, and grab me by the ears, saying, "Listen up, Sue!" But very rarely is it so forceful.

To encourage the still, small voice to speak, I begin each writing session with a simple practice in which I call in my guardian angels, muse, and any other helper beings who want to be a part of the circle. The components of the practice are straightforward: the invitation, a prayer about opening myself to my own and angelic wisdom and intuition, and a thank-you for being present with me. Sometimes I feel little shivers that, to me, announce the presence of my angels and helper beings. Often, however, physical assurances are lacking, and I must simply trust they have answered my request. Because writing is such a solitary endeavor, it's a comfort to believe I'm accompanied by helpers from a higher realm.

On days when writing is laborious and my mind and heart feel as if they are unsuccessfully trying to surface from a vat of gelatin, it's often because I've forgotten the practice. Not being as fluent and creative as I desire alerts me to the fact that quieting down before writing, taking time to ask for help, and then giving thanks for it is a tried-and-true way for me to be better attuned to the still, small voice of wisdom.

The voice of wisdom is inherent within us and willing to guide us when we stop to listen. Of course, there are times when we feel we've been still as stone, and the still, small voice is *still* too quiet to hear. When this happens, the challenge is to practice quieting your mind anyway. Stopping and asking, quieting and listening, trusting and waiting. Waiting is difficult but worth the effort because a quiet, uncluttered mind is a natural antenna for whispers of wisdom from within.

Practice...

✳ Take a few cleansing and quieting breaths. Even if you do not hear or sense it, give thanks for the still, small voice of wisdom within.

✳ As you continue to breathe softly, use your in breath to say, "I open to...," and your out breath to say, "the wisdom within."

Throughout your day...

✳ Affirm that the still, small voice of wisdom is alive within you.

A quiet mind hears whispers of wisdom.

Activating Awe

Cathy, a wonderful young woman I know, approached me at church and enthusiastically asked, "Have you ever been to Hawaii?" Since I lived there for five years early in my marriage, the answer was affirmative. "Omigosh, it was beautiful!" she raved. "My awe-o-meter was off the charts while I was there!"

I loved Cathy's reference to her "awe-o-meter." And I was struck by the fact that I hadn't been awed in a while. Did that mean awesome things had disappeared from my life? No. What it did mean was that I'd gotten too caught up in distractions and mind mucking to recognize anything as awe inspiring. Cathy's comments made me aware that I hadn't been paying attention to the beauty around me. To help bring myself back to mindfully registering my wonder and reverence for the world, I took my little dog, Lily, for an awe-o-meter walk that afternoon.

Lily's a great companion for such a journey because she is awed by each and every smell along the way, which gives me plenty of time to open my eyes, quiet my mind, and actually *see* what is present. Even though Mother Nature was in winter mode during our walk, there was much to inspire awe. The resident blue heron showed herself, a muskrat swam among some ducks, and Lily herself made me smile and feel incredibly grateful for the love this little ragamuffin has inspired in my life and my husband's. I saw more on that conscious awe-o-meter walk than I had in many, many previous walks.

J. Krishnamurti says, "To understand the immeasurable, the mind must be extraordinarily quiet, still." Naturally, none of us is going to have a quiet mind all of the time. Nor should we even expect that of ourselves. However, we can choose minutes in which to be quietly and consciously mindful of experiences, people, ideas, and loveliness that bring a sense of awe and reverence to our hearts. Seeing the immeasurable beauty and wonder in our own neighborhoods can be awesome in its own right. We don't have to go to Hawaii to have our awe-o-meters rocket off the charts.

Practice...

✳ Choose to walk somewhere you normally drive. Really look at and register the beauty you see.

✳ Tour one of the rooms in your own home. Become aware of your precious objects. Remember their significance. Touch the surfaces of furniture and memorabilia, feel the textures, allow your hands and eyes to caress and admire them. Awesome, right?

Throughout your day...

✳ Activate your awe-o-meter at least twice a day.

**A few mindful moments can
make an awesome difference.**

Saying Yes to Receptivity

If you've ever thought of someone and they call soon after, or you've been thinking about a topic and the person you're with begins talking about the same subject, you've experienced what I call "energy arcs" between people. We are more receptive to the arcs of energy between ourselves and others when our minds are quiet and free from static. A quiet mind gives us the readiness to receive impressions or ideas from others, our own higher selves, and the universe. We, however, need to supply the willingness to receive and register intuitive nudges, wisdom whispers, and creative urges.

A quiet, receptive mind is a friendly mind, interested in and aware of nuances within ourselves and others that a cluttered mind doesn't have the time or inclination to notice. Openness and accessibility are also qualities of a quiet mind. We are drawn to people who are interested in us and open with us, and whose ideas and emotions are accessible and readily expressed. In other words, women love to truly and genuinely *connect* with others. One reason we value our women friends so much is that they also want to make meaningful connections and are usually good at it.

Many years ago both of my sons were seriously injured within days of each other. The boys' injuries were dream-shattering for them and, consequently, for me also. After days of emotional turmoil, my husband and I capped off the trauma by having a big fight. Stunned from one too many blows, I fled the house to seek solace from my dear friend Bonnie. Even though I hadn't taken the time to call, I desperately hoped she'd be home. She was and provided the consolation I needed. Later she told me that she had had plans but "felt me coming" and stayed home to meet me. Bonnie was receptive to the energy arc between us and, consequently, was where she needed to be when I needed her.

Not only does being receptive help us be better friends and lovers, it also gives us a clearer conduit to the realms of the Divine. I believe many forms of help and inspiration hover around us waiting to be called upon. Maybe the energy arc between Bonnie and myself was really an angel tapping her on the shoulder. No matter what our individual beliefs, help, inspiration, and intuition *do* come into our minds. Our task is to say yes to receptivity by quieting our minds.

Practice...

✳ Set the intention to be aware of energy arcs between you and those you love.

✳ When intuition speaks, listen. When inspiration strikes, act.

Throughout your day...

✳ Take a moment to breathe in quietness and invite receptivity.

The quieter you become, the more you can hear.
—Ram Dass

Opening to Spaciousness

Chinese philosopher Lao-tzu, who is known as the father of Taoism, assures us that "to the mind that is still, the whole universe surrenders." The idea of the whole universe surrendering to me is a bit too daunting, so my interpretation of Lao-tzu's message is that living with a quiet mind promises life and love will flow more smoothly.

Stillness is an ever-present theme in mindfulness and meditation teachings—the core around which they circle. Meditation teachers advise that the stillness of meditation creates spaciousness, a roominess in which the mind can rest and find relief from the stories we tell ourselves about ourselves, our lives, and the obligations and responsibilities we carry. In my own practice, I've come to think of meditation as an oasis of stillness in the midst of everyday life. A sacred place where I find sanctuary from both the joy and sadness most days offer. A retreat in which there is nothing to do and no one to please, a spaciousness for simply being. A place to fall back in love with myself.

Because I find meditation such an oasis, you'd think I'd be disciplined enough to do it every day, but I'm sorry to say I'm not. I usually practice mindfulness each day, but often mindful moments are wedged in between activities or sleep cycles. And there are days when my mind is too full or too uneasy to be truly mindful. I'm learning to see these undisciplined, overfull, and worried times as part of my practice also—an opportunity to be gentle with myself even though I'm not being a good mindfulness meditation practitioner, or a good anything. So please don't be hard on yourself if you, too, wander away from your chosen path. Your ongoing task is to love yourself through all of life's detours.

In fact, being still enough to create the openness and generosity of heart to love yourself in the moment, is the greatest gift spaciousness has to offer. When you genuinely love and accept yourself, love naturally flows freely from you to all other beings and it does, indeed, feel as if the whole universe is surrendering to you.

Practice...

* Sit still a minute with no focus or agenda.

* Gently bring your attention to your breath, allowing it to rise and fall naturally.

* With each breath cycle, imagine yourself effortlessly expanding into spaciousness.

* Name the spaciousness "Love," and rest there.

Throughout your day...

* Imagine, and *feel* if possible, yourself at peace in a space of love.

Flowing steadily
From a spacious quiet mind,
Peace, love, harmony.

chapter 5

accepting what is

Mindfulness is simply being aware of what is happening right now without wishing it were different; enjoying the pleasant without holding on when it changes (which it will); being with the unpleasant without fearing it will always be this way (which it won't). —James Baraz

In a society that stresses being in control, self-reliance, and the belief that we create our own reality, the concept of mindful acceptance is a hard one to get our arms around. While I definitely have faith in the ideas of self-reliance and creating our own reality, I also believe that gracious acceptance of circumstances, emotions, and experiences is very often a necessary, though neglected, part of life's process.

For many years I was much better at resisting and attempting to control realities I didn't like than I was at gracefully accepting them. Although I was familiar with the adage "Go with the flow," I was an against-the-current swimmer. Eventually, it became apparent that *resistance is futile*, as Star Trek's Borg like to expound. For me, resistance magnified any pain I was feeling and, seemingly, locked me in the embrace of that which I resisted.

Before I could relax my grip on the fantasy that I might control anything other than my own thoughts, attitudes, and choices, I needed to stop equating acceptance with capitulation, victimization, and helplessness. With practice, it ultimately became apparent that acceptance actually *helped* me feel self-reliant and able to cocreate my reality with God. Surprisingly, I discovered that acceptance is empowering, whereas resistance is enervating. Of course, my knee-jerk reaction to some stimuli is still resistance and a desire to control, but more often than not, I can now start moving toward acceptance as soon as I become aware I've regressed to my old tightfisted, tight-hearted, uptight behavioral pattern.

Earning Angel Wings

During a brief hospital stay last year, I met a young male nurse who was a model of gracious acceptance. Dale and I made a sweet connection during our middle-of-the-night conversations, and he was definitely one of the silver linings in the whole experience. A brief story of his life unfolded as he took time to chat with me while taking care of nursing business. His story is bittersweet.

Dale was a second-year medical student when his wife was severely injured in an automobile accident. She survived the crash but was left with serious mental and physical challenges. Even if they'd had the money for him to stay in school, he said he would have dropped out because "our vows said for better or worse. We're a team. She'd do it for me. No big thing." He went on to explain he worked at night so he could be with his wife during the day, "You know, for company and to take her to doctor appointments and therapy sessions."

I was struck by how happy Dale was, so *okay* with and accepting of the dramatic turn his life had taken. To me, this man has earned his angel wings.

Dale's response to tragedy was so benevolent that I'm concerned your gut reaction might be "I couldn't possibly react in such a loving way," as mine was. In reality, we don't know how we will act and react until faced with specific experiences. Maybe you and I would also be angelic if placed in Dale's shoes.

Once again your task is to love and accept yourself whether you are mindfully and graciously accepting all that comes your way or miserably resisting each and every experience and feeling. I know I harp on the need for self-love, but it's because self-love is absolutely the bedrock of your life journey. With a foundation of acceptance, respect, and love for yourself, you have the stability, security, and courage to set about earning your angel wings in all areas of life.

Practice...

✳ If acceptance is particularly difficult for you, please treat yourself gently and start small.

✳ Choose one insignificant challenge to be accepting of—a slow checkout line, dirty socks on the floor, a computer glitch, and so on.

✳ Be aware of your body as you experience resistance, breathe into the areas that are tense, and encourage yourself to relax into acceptance.

Throughout your day...

✳ Notice resistance and consciously choose acceptance in its place. Because it usually takes a while for feelings to match intentions, please be patient with yourself.

Angel wings are earned one tiny feather at a time.

Giving Up Grumbling

As a therapist I believe a certain amount of catharsis is necessary for our mental and physical well-being. Built up energy must be expelled in useful ways or it has a tendency to turn inward and sour into illness, fear, or any number of destructive beliefs and expectations. That being said, I also know that consistent complaining can be unhealthy, habit-forming, and personality *de*forming. Grumbling and complaining erode your happiness as well as your ability to feel goodwill toward others. Grumbling births grouches. Grouches are hard to be around and not usually popular with themselves or anyone else.

As an antidote to the self-defeating habit of grumbling, Kansas City, Missouri, minister Will Bowen challenges his congregation—and, as it is evolving, much of the rest of the world—to stop complaining, criticizing, gossiping, and using sarcasm for twenty-one days straight in order to break the habit. "Complaining draws all of its essence from negativity," he explains. "When you complain, you typically do it to attract attention or sympathy. You're sending out this vibrational energy that you're a victim, and the universe responds with more negativity."

To help effect positive change, Rev. Bowen and his congregation provide purple bracelets to people who feel they could benefit from a reminder as they change a negative habit to a positive one. Wearers are to switch the bracelet from one hand to the other when they find themselves complaining, gossiping, criticizing, or using sarcasm, and after the switch—this is the hard part—start their twenty-one-day cycle over. At the end of an e-mail the other day, a friend wrote (with a smiley face), "I've changed my bracelet four-teen times during this one e-mail." Since he is definitely not a chronic complainer, I see both his humor and his e-mail as a constructive way to release a little pent-up energy.

Grumbling and acceptance rarely coexist.

Practice...

✳ Without judgment, notice when you complain and thank yourself for being aware.

✳ Mindfully and gently decide if it's good for you to continue thinking or speaking as you are, or if it would be better to change your thoughts and words. Act accordingly.

✳ At the end of the day, review each time you consciously gave up grumbling.

Throughout your day...

✳ Cancel grumbling with acceptance.

**Giving up grumpiness is beneficial
to your health and welfare.**

Choosing the Parts You Play

William Shakespeare assured us that "all the world's a stage, and all the men and women merely players. They have their exits and their entrances, and one man in his time plays many parts..." Frequently, I think it's healthy and fun to consider life a stage upon which we play out different story lines. While there are some immutable parameters within which your dramas and comedies are acted out—gender, nationality, health, quality of parenting received, and physical appearance, to name a few—it is within your power to choose your response to life's scripts and, in so doing, pick the best aspect of yourself for the current part you need to play.

For years I had a penchant for miscasting myself as the heroine tied to the railroad tracks, underappreciated Cinderella, or Brunhilda-the-Terrible in life's dramas. Choosing stronger, more adult facets of myself to take center stage now keeps both my Drama Queen and Victim characters from acting on their addiction to the adrenalin of drama.

Does choosing how to act and who to be complement accepting what is? I think so. Acceptance does not mean allowing yourself to be run over by circumstances; it is often simply nonresistance. Therefore, by becoming aware of the script that has been tossed metaphorically in your lap and saying, "Ah, so here is the playbill for this evening," you are accepting the situation with equanimity. From a place of balance and acceptance, you have the power to choose the character within you that best fits the role you're asked to play in the moment. For instance, if a family member is ill, the best role might be Tenacious Medical Advocate. When a friend or child is emotionally wounded, your part could be that of Safe, Supportive Shoulder. Ideally, we *accept* what has come our way and then mindfully and wisely *choose* to respond from the most appropriate actor available in our internal cast of characters.

Practice...

✳ Just for fun, think of a current life situation and choose a character within you that can handle the scenario well.

✳ Act the part, being mindful of how it feels to express this aspect of yourself.

✳ Thank this part of yourself and continue to use the role if it works.

Throughout your day...

✳ Accept what comes your way and mindfully choose who responds.

✳ Have fun with it.

You are the star of your life.

Waiting for Ripeness

Allowed to mature naturally, fruits and vegetables ripen in their own time according to the type of soil, sun, and rain they enjoy. Forcing them to grow in accordance with our schedules and desires by placing them in a hothouse seems an apt metaphor for many of the demands we place on ourselves. We expect to become proficient in everything from computers to parenting skills quickly and effortlessly and can feel like failures if we don't know what to do *right now* when faced with a crucial decision. It's as if we expect our own maturation process to resemble the instant-access technology we rely on. It ain't gonna happen.

The sooner we accept the fact that time ripens all things— especially we human beings—the more calm, patient, and peaceful we will become. Just as fruits and vegetables need the sun and rain to come to fruition, we need and deserve to ripen slowly and fully in the light of our own acceptance. Poet Rainer Maria Rilke encourages us to "have patience with everything unresolved in your heart, and try to love the questions themselves."

Rilke's statement is an important one for me. Reading it encourages me to relax into the unknown, trusting that ripeness will happen in the fullness of time.

As I write about ripeness, the difference between vine-ripened and hothouse tomatoes keeps coming into my mind. I was raised in hot, humid Missouri, where I learned to love garden-fresh tomatoes. But I like them peeled. Not a problem for vine-ripened tomatoes. Their skins slide off easily. However, the best way to get skin off of hothouse tomatoes is to first dunk them in boiling water, but they still don't taste like "real" tomatoes. Hmm ... How often have I gotten myself in hot water by doing or saying something before the time was ripe or expecting myself to be or do what I was not yet fully ripened into and ready for? Quite a few times, actually, and the forced, accelerated results were not as delicious as they might have been had I trusted that ripeness would come in due time.

Practice...

✳ Lovingly become aware of areas in which you are pushing yourself faster than you can comfortably and competently go.

✳ Take a few slow, deep breaths, and relax into the idea of ripeness.

Throughout your day...

✳ Ask yourself if this idea, decision, action, or emotion is really fully ripe. If not, wait, trusting that time and intention ripens all things.

The sweetness of a ripe fruit is worth the wait.

Making Heaven of Hell

Sorrow, loss, and physical pain are facts of life. Some of us are fortunate enough to experience only a little, and some of us seem to have far more than our share of each. How we respond to pain and sadness is entirely up to us. John Milton made a wonderful point when he said, "The mind is its own place and in itself can make a Heaven of Hell, a Hell of Heaven."

My former client, Patty, was the queen of making a heaven of hell. Patty's husband was killed by "friendly fire" in a military action, leaving her with five children to raise on very little money. On top of that, Patty endured painful bouts of fibromyalgia *and* her youngest child had Down's syndrome. She came to see me because, as she said, "I get a little blue sometimes and just wanted an adult to talk to…" A little blue! I couldn't even imagine surviving under such conditions. But survive Patty and all her kids did. I was struck by the fact that Patty made at least a passing reference to how lucky she was in each of our sessions. It was no mystery who was inspiring whom in our meetings.

Patty made me wonder why some people seem to stumble into little potholes when faced with pain or sadness whereas others plummet into the deepest craters. Working with other clients who tended to fall into hellish craters helped me understand a few of the differences between those who "potholed" and those who "cratered." Here are some examples:

Potholers	Craterers
Concentrate on staying in the here and now	Worry about the future
Consciously work on accepting what is	Believe things shouldn't be as they are
See themselves as survivors	View themselves as victims
Try to have positive thoughts	Are plagued by fearful thoughts

Fear and resistance create craters.

Practice...

∗ When experiencing fear bring yourself into the safety of the here and now by concentrating on each breath.

∗ Change hellish thoughts to heavenly ones.

Throughout your day...

∗ Find small ways to feel lucky

Heaven or hell; we choose.

Remembering to Exhale

I once rode a roller coaster in Las Vegas designed, I'm sure, by a demented person for the purpose of supporting the chiropractors in town. Its twists and turns, jerks and lunges were more than most human bodies could withstand. Except for screaming, I held my breath through the entire battering. In pain and dripping adrenaline, I staggered off. Taking one look at me, my definitely smarter, nonriding spouse said anxiously, "Breathe, Susie!" As I huffed out the breath I'd been holding, my body began releasing accumulated tension through trembling.

Life is sometimes like that roller coaster—filled with real and imagined danger, crammed with unexpected twists and turns, and resulting in stress, anxiety, and pain. When faced with danger, all breathing beings first gasp, then hold their breath, then breathe very shallowly. Only when the perceived danger has passed do they exhale completely and begin returning to normal breathing patterns.

Even though it is instinctive behavior, holding our breath or breathing shallowly does not help us function optimally. Breath is the life force. Deprived of it, our brains slow down and our bodies and emotions panic and shout, "Red alert!" Holding your breath is a bodily expression similar to emotionally grasping tightly something you fear losing. Being aware of your breathing, remembering to exhale, and resuming normal breathing as soon as possible is an effective way to accept the reality of right now.

Exhaling brings us the relief of relaxing, letting go, and releasing pent-up tension. Tears often have the same cleansing effect, as the Jewish proverb "What soap is for the body, tears are for the soul" assures us. Actually, tears also cleanse the body. Science has proven that tears shed as a result of difficult feelings, such as grief and anger, contain toxins, while tears flowing from positive feelings do not. How deeply and rhythmically you breathe is a conscious, mindful choice, as is allowing yourself the release of tears.

Practice...

✳ Sit quietly with your eyes closed and gently focus on breathing in through your nose and out through your mouth for two or three minutes.

✳ Even if it is hard, give yourself permission to release any tears waiting to be shed. (In order to encourage tears, I may repeat "No!" several times and even pound on my bed.)

✳ In crisis, remember to breathe in *and* out.

Throughout your day...

✳ Consciously even out your breath. Inhale to the count of five … Exhale to the count of five…

Both exhaling and crying make way for the clean, fresh, and new.

Using AOL

If we could all follow Monty Python's advice in *Life of Brian* when they sing, "When you chew on life's gristle, don't grumble, just whistle...," we'd be in fat city, so to speak. But often the worries and stresses of life's gristle get us down and seduce us into thinking we can somehow make everything better by finding ways to control the situation. Unfortunately, continuously chewing on a challenge usually doesn't solve it but simply makes it bigger and bigger and harder and harder to digest. Reminds me of chewing liver ... ugh.

When we let worries consume us, they become the matrix around which our lives revolve. They own us. Because I know so well how easy it is to get lost in a maze of worry, I came up with AOL, a system that helps me find my way out.

Aware: Become aware of what you are gnawing on and how you feel about it. For instance, I can lose sleep worrying about my adult kids.

Observe: Without judgment, observe how your worries and concerns trap you in an endless cycle of "what ifs," "I shoulds," and possibly some "ain't it awfuls." Worry about my kids takes me out of the here and now and into places where I have no control. Nor should I.

Let go: Depending on what your heart resonates with, there are innumerable ways to release gristle. I often use affirmation, prayer, visualization, and ritual.

To let go of kid concerns, I ask for help releasing worry and verbalize what I know to be true of my children by affirming their strength, goodness, wisdom, and kindness. I visualize them happy. If my heart still aches, it's ritual time. Recently, I threw leaves symbolizing my concerns into the stream behind our house. Fear, lack of trust, and sadness all rode the current downstream. As they disappeared, I gave thanks for the idea of letting go and for my children, no matter where they were in the moment. It worked.

Practice...

✳ Use AOL—be aware, observe, let go—when worry consumes you.

Throughout your day...

✳ Remind yourself that "this too shall pass."

Love yourself as you move toward and beyond letting go.

Giving Grace Your Hand

Grace is goodness and respect given freely and unconditionally. A sense of divine love and protection bestowed on us when we need strength and renewal. Grace helps us know we are not alone and believe we are cared for and cherished. Grace is a drink of clear, clean water in the desert.

The grace of God, the grace of friendship, the grace of pets, the grace of competent and compassionate professionals, the grace of nature, the grace of hope, and the grace of angels surround us in all situations and circumstances. We, however, need to believe in the potential for grace and reach out our hearts to accept it from all who offer its solace and support.

I love the following assurance by author and theologian Frederick Buechner "The grace of God means something like: 'Here is your life. You might never have been, but you *are* because the party wouldn't have been complete without you. Here is the world. Beautiful and terrible things will happen. Don't be afraid. I am with you. Nothing can ever separate us. It's for you I created the universe. I love you.'

There's only one catch. Like any other gift, the gift of grace can be yours only if you'll reach out and take it.

Maybe being able to reach out and take it is a gift too" (1999, 139).

Whether or not you can reach out and take the gift of grace is determined by your state of mind. Not believing grace is accessible or feeling as if you are not worthy of receiving it blocks the flow of grace naturally longing to come your way.

Feelings elicited by the gift of grace manifest differently for each of us. Grace can feel as if you're enfolded in a loving hug. Or it may mean that hope and a belief in possibilities break through a mind shrouded in depression. Grace may unstick what was stuck in or around you. And, miraculously, grace may give you the gift of *really knowing* you are loved and lovable.

Practice...

* Become aware of your feelings about the availability of grace.

* If you doubt the gift of grace, who within you doubts? Ask internal doubters what they want and need from you. Grant their wishes.

* Enhance belief by breathing in slowly, saying, "Thank you...," and breathing out, "...for the gift of grace."

* In times of need, reach out to grace by breathing in "I accept and welcome..." and breathing out "...the gift of grace."

Throughout your day...

* Make a point to notice grace everywhere.

**Swaying with the wind
A willow exemplifies
Grace-filled acceptance.**

overflowing from an open heart

An open heart bridges heaven and earth.

Being able to open your heart to yourself and others and *re*open it when it snaps shut in the face of danger, despair, and disillusionment may be the greatest challenge of your lifetime. Because we are vulnerable humans prone to defensiveness, opening our hearts is an ongoing endeavor. With a genuine desire to keep your heart open as well as a deep and accepting understanding of how difficult it can be, you can be openhearted more often than not.

Earlier this year my mood was as bleak as the postblizzard streets were ugly and hazardous. Things had not been going my way, and I felt like a teeth-clenching, overstimulated, closed-hearted witch whose every nerve was exposed and jangling. Driving to an appointment in town, I begged, "Please, angels, God, all my guides and guardians, I need help opening my heart again!" Nothing happened. No miracle, no warm, fuzzy feelings, only my continual reassurance to myself that awareness is the first step toward change, and I was painfully aware of my pinched heart.

While maneuvering the ice-clogged streets, I saw a police car blocking a right turn lane. As I approached, the reason for the car's position became apparent. A policewoman was gently and cautiously helping an elderly woman navigate the treacherously slippery crosswalk. This vignette of kindness caused tears to flow and was a wonderful answer to my prayer. It was the beginning of my heart's much-needed thaw.

Until we are fully enlightened, our hearts will cycle between open and closed, frozen and flowing. To assure more opening than closing, it is extremely important to maintain a climate of gentle understanding toward yourself during *both* frozen and flowing times.

Starting a Kindness Revolution

I like to think it's no accident that our species is called human-kind. Human*kind*! What if we—just you and me—made a commitment to mindfully integrate kindness into each and every day of our lives? We would start a kindness revolution. Let's do it. Let's become the proverbial pebbles in the pond and send ripples of kindness out into the world each day. Those whose hearts are touch by our kindness will, hopefully, be encouraged to pass it on, and a revolution of much-needed kindness will have begun. Let's live up to our name by evolving into its implication—humans who are consistently kind.

In his wonderfully friendly and openhearted way, the Dalai Lama is already a kindness revolutionary. He states, "This is my simple religion. There is no need for temples; no need for complicated philosophy. Our own brain, our own heart is our temple; the philosophy is kindness." One of the blessings of believing in a philosophy of kindness is that kindness opens the hearts of both giver and receiver.

Another great philosopher, Winnie the Pooh, is also a member of the kindness ranks. He explains to a friend in the Thousand Acre Wood, "Just because an animal is large, it doesn't mean he doesn't want kindness; however big Tigger seems to be, remember that he wants as much kindness as Roo." Winnie's lesson is a good one to remember. No matter how big and tough someone looks, they want and need kindness as much as we do. As we start our powerful, heart-opening, and heartwarming revolution of kindness, what better companions can we have than the Dalai Lama and Winnie the Pooh?

Practice...

✳ Think big. We *can* have a huge influence.

✳ Act small. Each act of kindness, no matter how small, makes a big difference.

✳ Help yourself make a habit of integrating kindness into each day by posting a reminder like "Be Kind" where it is easily seen.

✳ Pause before acting or speaking and ask yourself, "What is kind in this situation?"

✳ Choose kindness.

✳ Give yourself a pat on the back in celebration of your own kindness and goodness. (Doing so boosts your belief in yourself and makes it easier to create a habit of kindness.)

Throughout your day...

✳ Commit conscious acts of kindness.

Being kind in thought, word, and deed opens your heart.

Finding Freedom in Forgiveness

Nothing slams your heart shut more resoundingly than holding a grudge, nursing a grievance, stewing in resentment, or resisting what is or was. Not being able to forgive binds us to the original wound and to the one who wounded us. Remaining in a state of anger or hurt and—no matter how secretly—desiring revenge is akin to lugging around an internal cauldron of boiling bile hoping it will somehow scald the *other* person. It won't. But building up the bile of nonforgiveness sure does hurt you. Holding on to an injustice blocks the flow of life's good energy, depletes your immune system, and makes laughter, love, and joy very difficult to feel. Ironically, while the lack of forgiveness greatly impacts us, it has little or no effect on the person with whom we are upset.

The idea that forgiveness is the best revenge could well be true. Forgiveness frees us from the past, empowers us to move on, and allows us to regain the ability to make fun, loving, and light-filled choices. Because of the enormous benefits to the one who forgives, forgiveness could almost be seen as a selfish act. It's definitely a self-loving act.

Which brings me to the fundamental aspect of forgiveness: the necessity of forgiving yourself. Forgiving ourselves includes making amends to whomever we have offended or hurt, learning from our mistakes, and mindfully avoiding doing the same things again. Forgiving yourself entails accepting the person you were at the time by realizing you would have acted or spoken differently if you'd known how. Most of us need to forgive ourselves for things done or said unwittingly or thoughtlessly. However, if you *consciously* wound others, it can indicate deep-seated anger and injuries that may be beyond your ability to heal on your own. If this is true for you, please give yourself the gift of therapy.

Practice...

✳ Without judgment, become aware of anyone you need to forgive, including yourself.

✳ As you breathe deeply and rhythmically, allow an image of the person to come into your mind's eye. Ask for divine love to flow into and through you toward them and silently say, "I forgive you and release my feelings of _____."
(Visualizing the person as an innocent toddler often helps forgiveness flow. This technique can be especially valuable when forgiving parents.)

✳ Make amends if needed.

Throughout your day...

✳ Affirm your commitment to forgive.

✳ Create personal rituals of release and forgiveness that bring you peace.

Forgiveness is freedom.

Being a Friend

Having trusted friends is a must. Undoubtedly, most of our closest and dearest friends will be women because we all want and need the same kind of heart connection and honest sharing of feelings.

True friends *see* who we really are, *hear* our words and the feelings behind them, *hold* us in the safe harbor of their embrace, and *accept* us as we are. Good friends mirror our best back to us, forgive our worst, and believe we will evolve into wise, wacky, and wonderful old broads. Dear friends give us their undivided attention, encourage us to laugh, and entice us into silliness. And we do the same for them.

A true friend gives us the courage to be ourselves because we know she is *with* us always and in all ways. In the safety of such friendships, our hearts can fully open.

I'm not sure how I would have survived the collapse of my first marriage without my women friends. One ranted and raved with me on the night I found out about my husband's betrayal, and together we pretend-planned how to maim him in the most painful way possible. We howled with laughter and with hurt, indignation, and downright terror on my part. And then she tucked me in bed. Throughout the long process of disentangling, my friends encouraged me, comforted me, and finally kicked me in the buns and lovingly—with some well-founded impatience—told me to get on with it. They were right, and I followed their advice.

Ah, now the harder questions: Are you a trustworthy and devoted friend to *yourself*? Do you treat yourself with as much love and support as you do your three dearest friends? I would not have been able to answer yes to those questions before my divorce. My self-esteem was in the toilet and my fear levels off the charts. By continuing to befriend me when I felt like such a pitiful loser, women—and a few wonderful men—helped me begin to believe in myself in a way I never had before. Learning to be my own dear friend was possibly the biggest blessing I gained from that painful experience.

Practice...

✳ Consciously choose to treat yourself as well as you do dear friends, even if it feels unnatural.

✳ Tell a friend how much you appreciate them.

Throughout your day...

✳ Nurture friendships with kindness, understanding, empathy, and laughter.

✳ Connect with a friend in a small or large way.

Befriend yourself and you naturally befriend others.

Knowing You Are Lovable and Loved

Trusting that you are lovable and loved is one of the best ways to become openhearted. Feeling lovable and loved on the inside makes it easier to express love outwardly. If feeling loved and believing you are lovable is difficult for you, you can begin moving toward more positive beliefs and emotions by accepting, loving, and healing the child you were. She lives within you and may still fear she is not worthy of love.

Until the age of six or seven, children think the entire world revolves around them and, consequently, that they cause anything that happens in their sphere. If a child received only unconditional love and could always rely on adults and the world not to disappoint her, that would be great. But such childhoods are rare. In the real world, things go awry and people are imperfect. By believing they cause all the bad stuff, children can come to the conclusion that they must be flawed and unlovable.

While you know intellectually you were not to blame for the circumstances of your childhood, your inner little girl may carry residual shame from believing she was somehow bad. For instance, Shanti, a beautiful and talented young woman I know, can lose sight of the woman she has become when the child she was is triggered by fear, failure, or insecurity. As the youngest child of a narcissistic, attacking mother, Shanti became her mother's favorite target. Because she could not do anything well enough and could never count on her unpredictable mother, Shanti felt unsafe and insecure throughout her formative years.

Because of the depths of her wounds, it isn't easy for Shanti to feel lovable now; however I believe it will be natural for her one day because she is absolutely dedicated to healing her inner child and living as a strong, loving woman today.

A wounded heart is vulnerable yet capable of great compassion. All of us are wounded to some degree, and each of us has the ability to heal and open her heart. An open heart is a powerful emissary for all that is loving and good. Each open heart increases beauty and compassion in the cosmos.

Practice...

✳ Quiet your mind by focusing solely on your breath for a few minutes.

✳ Visualize your inner little girl as happy, playful, and receiving all she wants and deserves.

✳ Bless any negative thoughts or images that arise. Bless them and let them go. Gently return to the here and now of your breath.

Throughout your day...

✳ Love your inner child.

You are God's beloved daughter, completely lovable and constantly loved.

Giving Gratitude a Go

Gratitude is the golden key to opening your heart. Being grateful is paying attention to and appreciating life's treasures. Reveling in the blessings and riches life offers creates feelings of well-being, love, abundance, and delight. Highlighting and celebrating the positive encourages your heart to unfurl, much like warm sunlight prompts a flower to open.

As a sage once said, "Gratefulness creates great fullness." From great fullness, we can easily and effortlessly overflow onto Mother Earth and all her children. Giving from overflow is a gift without strings or expectations attached, whereas giving out of obligation when we feel drained can deplete us even more and be laced with exhaustion, resentment, or anger.

Paradoxically, when we feel empty and purposeless, selfless giving is often exactly what we need to do in order for our hearts to experience great fullness. Giving to others who are less fortunate or are going through a hard time activates gratitude within us—gratitude for our own blessings, for being able to be of service—and awe and gratitude for the inspiration provided by people who survive adversity. If you are feeling drained or empty, quiet your mind and gently pay attention to your needs. In the calm quietness, clarity can come, and you will know whether reaching out or going within is needed to provide balance right now.

As a mindfulness practice, or to fill yourself up when running on empty, try giving gratitude a go. Having an attitude of gratitude reminds us of our source and reconnects us to the essence of spirit. As a French proverb explains, "Gratitude is the heart's memory." Awakening to gratitude and noticing all you have to be thankful for places you in the embrace of the Divine, where your heart can open and overflow as naturally as a spring flows from its source.

Practice...

✳ Set your intention to give gratitude a go each day.

✳ Before getting out of bed in the morning, be grateful for another day of life. Follow with a simple prayer, such as:

Thank you for today. Please help me handle it with grace, gratitude, happiness, and strength.

✳ During the day, consciously replace fear-based thoughts with ones of gratitude and joy.

✳ Before drifting off to sleep at the end of the day, think of at least two people, experiences, or things for which you are grateful. Reexperience the sweet feelings as deeply as you can.

Throughout your day...

✳ Each hour, take a moment to fully notice something for which you are grateful.

Gratitude fills a thirsty heart to overflowing.

Expecting Good

Although intangible, thoughts, expectations, and beliefs are powerful, magnetic realities drawing to us energy and experiences that match what we send out. Expecting good is issuing an invitation to the universe to send more good your way. For instance, if you expect your day to be a good one, chances are it will be. If you expect it to be lousy, the law of attraction often makes sure your expectation is met.

There are times when believing good is already here or expecting it is on the way doesn't seem to make any noticeable difference in your life. Patience is needed because *our* time and God's time often differ. Also, God's way of providing our good can certainly look different than we expect it to. In fact, it sometimes appears as if God loves a scavenger hunt and delights in hiding my good deep in what, at first, appears to be manure.

If I had known a psychotherapy practice and a writing career would evolve from the struggles life generously provided, would I have resisted the pain less? I don't know, but from the wisdom of hindsight, I do know that adversity made me a stronger woman and provided the impetus to create two careers I'm passionate about and hope help the world a little.

It's much easier to expect good when you believe God (or please insert your own name for the Divine) is benevolent and wants only good for you. I've grown to agree with author Max Lucado's opinion about how much God loves us. He says, "If God had a refrigerator, your picture would be on it" (2006). The optimist I've become intentionally chooses to expect a good outcome, an important lesson, and an opportunity for inspiration to come from all occurrences. When I can't do that, I pay attention to my breath and stay safely in the present moment as much as possible.

Practice...

✳ Quietly become aware of your breath.

✳ Easily and gently deepen your breath.

✳ Return to normal breathing and imagine breathing in and out from your heart center.

✳ On the in breath affirm, "God loves me." On the out breath, affirm, "And so do I."

✳ With your hands faceup on your lap, request, "Please help me cradle, not clutch, each person, feeling, and experience that comes my way today."

Throughout your day...

✳ Be aware of and appreciate even the smallest good that comes to you.

Expect, notice, and accept good.

Being a Cheerleader

Recently, while pondering my purpose in life, an absurd thought popped into my head: "You're a cheerleader." No, wait, that answer is about fifty years and a whole lot of flexibility too late ... But the more I thought about being a cheerleader, the better I liked the idea. Don't you love to be cheered on in your endeavors? Isn't it great to receive a rousing "Atta girl!" when you score a success? And doesn't it help relieve the feeling of being all alone when a supportive friend urges, "Defense! Defense!" if you're being maligned or mistreated?

Aware of my own yearning to be cheered on when a girl and young woman, somewhere along the line I made a conscious decision to cheer on others. At first, I had to remind myself to applaud and approve of others and, yes, to consistently and nonjudgmentally give myself the accolades I'd felt deprived of growing up and in my first marriage.

Luckily, several of the women I was close to at the time also needed cheerleaders. We supported each other to the point of sometimes yelling, "Standing ovation! Standing ovation!" which meant the woman who wanted and needed cheering was to stand and bow in response to our shouts of approval. Giving and receiving standing ovations was rowdy fun and surprisingly rewarding for both applauder and applaudee— probably because our hearts open more fully when we help others feel good about themselves.

Accentuating the positive by seeing and appreciating the good in others, in yourself, and in the world around you draws additional goodness to you. In his newsletter, meditation teacher and author James Baraz agrees that cheerleading can call forth goodness when he writes, "We have great power to draw out the goodness from others if we look for it. Try looking for what is good in others and life around you. [Have] your radar out for what you appreciate about them. Most people will sense this very easily and will relax around you as well as let their goodness more naturally shine" (2007).

Practice...

* Pay attention to your desire for approval and provide it unstintingly. It's perfectly okay to give yourself a standing ovation.

* Look for the good in others and shower them with appreciation, encouragement, and applause.

* "Listen and attend with the ear of your heart," as Saint Benedict urges.

Throughout your day...

* Find reasons to celebrate yourself and others.

Illuminated by the light of appreciation and approval, we shine.

Acting Lovingly

Love takes many forms: romantic, physical, altruistic, parental, familial, and impersonal, to name just a few. Love emanates from the center of your heart, and scientists now know that the heart is *the* most powerful organ in your body, both physically and energetically. As the highest form of heart energy, love is amazingly powerful. When we learn to choose what feels right in our hearts rather than what is logical to the mind, we will change the world in transformative and healing ways.

Two women I know have started transforming their worlds already. Anne's motto is "Love: Be it. Say it. Do it." As a survivor of cancer, she has honed what is important down to one thing: Love. To the best of her ability, she says it, does it, and is learning to be it more each day. Colleen concentrates on opening her heart and spreading love by asking, "What would Love do?" when faced with almost any question or action. I might add, "What is the *kind* response, action, or attitude for this time and setting?"

In part 1, I spoke about the insight progression our practices were designed to facilitate. It looks like this:

Insight ——> Awareness ——> Action

While it's wonderful to be mindful about asking what Love would do, it's only the first step. Asking gives you *insight* about what would be loving, *awareness* lets you know how you feel about the insight gained. Can you happily follow your heart's advice or do you feel resistant about heeding love's counsel? It really doesn't matter which it is; the crucial step is the next one. *Choosing to act* in a loving manner, no matter how you feel.

Interestingly, the energy of love is so powerful that it often boomerangs back to us, creating warm and fuzzy feelings even when we act from choice rather than feeling. Choosing an act of love can open your heart to the feelings of love.

Practice...

✳ Set an intention to act lovingly.

✳ Before reacting to a situation, take a few mindful breaths. Ask, "What would love do?" *Listen* to your heart.

✳ If still in doubt, give yourself the gift of time and acceptance. Breathe gently into your heart whenever thoughts of the dilemma come to mind, and relax into the awareness that, in the fullness of time, you will know how love wants to act through you.

Throughout your day...

✳ Choose to be, say, and do love.

Opening your heart,
A gift of mindfulness that
Spreads loving-kindness.

generating
soft power

At the center of your being you have the answer; you know who you are, and you know what you want.
—Lao-tzu

s bearers and givers of life and the core around which our families revolve, women are incredibly strong and amazingly powerful. Some of you probably recognized and claimed your innate strength and influence more gracefully than I did. When I began gaining a sense of empowerment, I also noticed myself growing a tougher-than-necessary shell. It was as if I felt the need for a steel exoskeleton to house my newfound power and hold me upright in the face of opposition from those who preferred I remain acquiescent and malleable. I wasn't alone in my crustiness. Many of my newly assertive clients and friends were also experiencing unfamiliar and uncomfortable tight-jawed toughness.

The adage "When the student is ready, the teacher will appear" came true for me at a friend's croning ceremony, at which several women gathered to honor our friend who had attained the age and gathered the wisdom designating an elder, or "crone." During the ritual, the facilitator mentioned the term "soft power" and a light went on within me. In that moment, I realized I had sacrificed the soft-edged, openhearted, ready-to-embrace aspects of myself on the altar of empowerment. During that flash of insight, I also understood I could have both.

Softness and empowerment complement each other. However, soft power can be distorted by unfinished business, limiting beliefs, old wounds, and fear, for example. By mindfully and lovingly clearing away emotional debris and honoring our authentic selves, we can bless those we care about—and the world in general—by naturally generating and expressing the soft power that is our fundamental nature.

Tying Up Loose Ends

Unfinished business is psychic flotsam and jetsam. Niggling beliefs about what you should have done, regrets about what you did or didn't do, or lingering feelings about what was done *to* you drain energy from the here and now by flinging your attention into the future or sinking it back into the past. Since all life resides in the moment, fragments of unfinished business exhaust rather than empower you.

One of the most effective ways to tie up loose ends is to *do* what can be done to bring closure. If the taxes are due, complete them. If you need to make amends, do so. If emotional baggage is weighing you down or trapping you in the past, find a therapist or friend who can help you heal, release, and let go. Throughout the process of finishing business and freeing yourself from draining thoughts, support yourself with acceptance and appropriate action.

Because our minds tend to get in a groove and replay the "oldies and baddies"—like real or imagined failures, wounds, guilt, and resentments—we need to find ways to change the station and claim our innate soft power. Continually thinking about what makes us feel bad is an indication we have become overly attached to our personal stories and possibly even addicted to the adrenaline produced by rehashing them. Old stories and the accompanying feelings can become your false identity. However, changing obsessive thoughts, tying up loose ends, and letting go of the past can help you become the softly empowered woman you can be *now*.

The breath practice below is designed to help free your mind from the grasp of unfinished business. Noticing thoughts neutrally and immediately letting them go breaks the bonds of habitual thinking and helps you recognize your authentic self in the present moment.

Practice...

* With your eyes closed, focus solely on your breath. Breathe naturally.

* When thoughts come, acknowledge them with a neutral word such as "thinking." Immediately return your attention to your breath. (It's not unusual to repeat the process many times during a session.)

* Do not judge your practice as good or bad. Simply acknowledge yourself for doing it.

* The keys to success are practice and neutrality.

Throughout your day...

* Do small things to tie up loose ends.

This moment is your power point.

Accessing Body Wisdom

Wouldn't it be wonderful to have a wise and intuitive counselor available 24/7? You're in luck; you already have one. Your body! Our bodies carry ancient wisdom. We literally live within a temple of intuitive and instinctual wisdom. Sometimes we pay attention and access body wisdom; but unfortunately, the aphorism "Mrs. Smith lived a short distance from her body" is sadly true for many of us.

Bernie Siegel, noted author and physician, believes our bodies are far more complex and fascinating than we give them credit for and that many patients invite body wisdom and meaning to triumph over fear. Of the people who heal miraculously, Dr. Siegel says, "They focus on the meaning of their life and their divine essence and they live it. They do not project their problems onto others but seek to make a beautiful world and create goodness in their relationships" (1986, 12). The body and mind are inextricably linked; what affects one affects the other. Dr. Siegel puts it this way: "Our problem lies in our ability to think and worry." Negative thinking and worry stifle your body's natural inclination toward health and wisdom. In its ideal state, the body can be likened to clear, clean springwater flowing sweetly from the breast of Mother Earth. Even when contaminated with tainted substances, springwater will cleanse itself. Of course, a spring needs time free from contaminants in order to stay clean, just as our physical, emotional, mental, and spiritual selves need time free from dirty, disabling thoughts of fear and resentment in order to operate optimally.

Not only is your body a temple filled with wisdom, it is also the one vehicle that carries you through life. The physical vehicle needs upkeep, care, good food, exercise, water, medical attention, and time to rest and rejuvenate. The wisdom temple needs positive thoughts and attitudes to keep it clean and sparkly. Also, the body temple thrives best when attention is paid to its innate wisdom. Accessing the body's wisdom can be as simple as acknowledging the need for a nap and taking one, if possible, or as miraculous as transforming a life-threatening illness into a life well lived.

Practice...

* Direct your attention and breath to your body. Breathe deeply into areas that are experiencing pain, tightness, or discomfort of any kind.

* As you breathe into challenging areas, thank them for all they do for you. Imagine breathing relaxation and healing into those areas.

Throughout your day...

* Notice and listen to your body.

**Body wisdom:
notice early; honor immediately.**

Reeling in Projections

An excellent indicator of soft power is having the maturity to take responsibility for your own feelings and behavior. Denying what lives inside us does not make it go away. Unidentified and unresolved feelings slip into hiding, like snakes going under a rock, where they wait until provoked to strike out, generally with inappropriate and wounding behavior. Unfortunately, those struck are often our loved ones.

Walloping someone else over the head with your own issues is called *projection*. The act of projecting can be described by using the analogy of a movie projector. Unaware of the subject matter of a film or DVD, a projector automatically shines the contents onto a blank screen. The person with hidden issues is the projector, her buried feelings are the content of the film or DVD, and the person projected upon is the blank screen hit by others' pent-up energy.

My client Marg lovingly and responsibly cared for her father for months before his death. Her dad's generation believed real men were strong, silent, and always in charge. Because he was intelligent, handsome, and accomplished, he never felt the need to be aware of or heal his vulnerable feelings. Emotional wounds sustained in war were buried along with all others, including the fear of decline and death. As Marg's father become weaker and more dependent, the energy of unresolved issues began to erupt. Feelings hidden for years were projected onto Marg as *her* failures. Even though she understood the psychological underpinnings of the attacks, Marg was understandably devastated by them.

Because most of us are not yet fully enlightened, we will occasionally project onto others. However, we can reel in the vast majority of our projections by discovering, healing, and taking responsibility for hidden feelings. If you do wound someone by word or action, diligently search for and examine feelings of your own that might have provoked the behavior. Bring troublesome feelings into the light of awareness and, with love, work on transforming them. Mend relationships by acknowledging unfair projections and sincerely apologizing.

Practice...

* Before saying anything that could be hurtful, pause. Breathe ... Breathe ... Breathe...

* Pause a while longer. Breathe into your heart.

* Nonjudgmentally, ask, "Could this be about me?"

* If so, gently explore your feelings with the goal of understanding and transforming them.

Throughout your day...

* Project acceptance onto yourself and others.

Project the light of love into the world.

Valuing Authenticity Over Perfection

Authenticity is achievable; perfection is not. "Authentic" is defined as genuine, trustworthy, and *real*, whereas the definition for "perfect" is downright scary. It is conforming absolutely to the description or definition of an ideal type (Stepford wife, for instance?) without flaws, defects, or short-comings (a very special rose, maybe). By definition, no one I know is perfect, but many are authentic.

Empowered people realize that everyone has a balance of strengths and vulnerabilities, virtues and vices and, as a result, can calmly accept their own. In reality, accepting our strengths and virtues is sometimes harder than owning and expressing vulnerability and vice. But honoring good qualities is an indispensable step toward generating the soft power of authenticity. During insecure and unhappy times as a young woman, it was much easier for me to highlight my own lowlights, so to speak.

When trying to accept or alter parts of myself, I find it helpful to give them a persona, as if they were characters in today's life-play. For instance, an angry aspect of myself once showed up as an ancient Norsewoman, complete with metal breastplates and a huge sword. "Brunhilda" made me chuckle and helped me temper the guilt I felt about being angry. Although I kept Brunhilda from wielding her sword maliciously, just knowing she carried it helped me stand up for myself when my anger was authentic and admirable.

My black-robed Judge subpersonality took the bench, grabbed her gavel, and banged it like a frustrated, glowering crow. My friend Juju made me laugh by offering all sorts of absurd suggestions about solving the dilemma I was upset about. Together, we permitted the Judge to express her melodramatic feelings without hurting anyone in the process. Letting my darker aspects rant for a little while, trying to find humor in them, and then mindfully reconnecting with lighter, nicer subpersonalities helps me stay authentic.

Practice...

* Make a list of your strengths and good qualities.

* While sitting for practice, breathe in, "I am [or have] ..." and breathe out one of your strengths or qualities. (As an example, breathe in "I have...," and breathe out "...a good sense of humor.")

* Pay attention to your less-acceptable parts. How can they complement the whole of your authentic self without being allowed to behave in hurtful ways?

* Become aware, enjoy, and alter, if necessary.

Throughout your day...

* Pay attention to the authenticity of your thoughts, words, and actions.

Get real.

Finding Your Voice

Finding their own unique voice is a huge issue for many women. As a teenager and twenty-something, I continually cleared my throat and felt I was choking much of the time. I was. Choking back words I thought people wouldn't like to hear, choking on feelings I didn't believe I could express, choking on self-judgment, choking on shoulds, have-tos, and fears. Not only were the reasons for clearing my throat limiting, the physical act itself was annoying and played havoc with some of my more promising dates.

In order to keep my throat clear, I needed to find my voice. To this day, learning to speak out in softly empowered ways is a continuing process for me. Anna, a client, had been working on finding her voice when, one day, she came bounding into my office bubbling with excitement. Hardly able to contain herself, she said, "Yesterday I was trying to express myself to my husband when he told me to crawl back into my hole." Pausing to laugh heartily, she proudly exclaimed, "I told him 'I can't. I filled it in!'" In daring to speak up, Anna felt exhilarated and empowered.

While many women have found their authentic voices and do not feel the need to silence themselves, some of us may still need a little encouragement. Not only does your voice express beliefs, ideas, and creativity unique to you, it also carries its own vibration. Using your voice as an expression of authenticity sends a vibration of honesty and trustworthiness into the atmosphere, where laws of nature cause those qualities to expand. Voices are powerful tools. Used mindfully and lovingly, your voice can have a healing impact both personally and globally.

Understandably, our voices can ring out with goodness and wisdom only when we trust that those qualities live within us. Meditation teacher Pema Chödrön uses her voice to invite us to be curious about ourselves in a light and loving way. "Meditation is a process of lightening up, of trusting the basic goodness of what we have and who we are, and realizing that any wisdom that exists, exists in what we already have. The key is to wake up, to become more alert, more inquisitive and curious about ourselves" (2001).

Just as a candle flame can be seen clearly in the darkness, one peaceful, loving voice can be heard amid even hate and horror. May our voices be among the peacemakers.

Practice...

✳ Place half of your attention on your breath and half on noticing aspects of yourself active now. Whether dark or light, healthy or wounded, nonjudgmentally notice the aspects as they surface.

✳ Gently acknowledge who needs to speak and who needs to learn to be quiet.

✳ Give yourself permission to find your voice.

Throughout your day...

✳ Speak your truth kindly and gently.

✳ Or choose to stay silent from integrity, not fear.

Your unique voice is important.

Erring on the Side of Generosity

Being generous is beneficial to both giver and receiver. In fact, the benefits gained from being generous are so great, it's fair to say generosity is self-loving as well as altruistic. A recipient of someone else's generosity gets items and attitudes valuable to them, whereas the giver is blessed by the positive feelings associated with openheartedness.

One form of generosity about which we've already spoken is kindness, but because I think it's impossible to tout kindness too often, I want to share two quotes I love that align generosity with kindness. The first is from author Robert Brault: "Today I bent the truth to be kind, and I have no regret, for I am far surer of what is kind than I am of what is true." Since I, too, am far surer of kindness than truth, this quote resonates with my heart. The next wisdom is from Ralph Waldo Emerson: "You can never do a kindness too soon, for you never know how soon it will be too late." Right! If you've ever delayed an act of kindness or generosity until it was too late, as I have, you know the sadness that clenches your heart as a result.

Believing the best about people and, therefore, giving them the benefit of the doubt, is another form of generosity that opens your heart. Believing in someone before all the facts are in is akin to being innocent until proven guilty. If you've experienced being misjudged, you can truly appreciate the value of judging others favorably. The other day, a woman I know accused me of something I would never even consider doing. "Don't you know me better than that?" I wanted to ask, but I didn't feel safe enough to do so. Although she later apologized, the experience remains a visceral lesson about how painful it is to be judged harshly and unfairly.

I am actually really thankful to have been given such an invaluable reminder to give others the benefit of the doubt. If you're reading this book in sequence, you know I have a hefty judge persona who can use all the lessons in slow judgment and fast forgiveness she can get.

To facilitate opening your heart—the seat of soft power—practice erring on the side of generosity.

Practice...

✳ Center and calm your body and mind by concentrating on your breath for a few minutes.

✳ If there is anyone you are judging or anyone you feel judged by, allow an awareness of them to float into your consciousness.

✳ Inhale divine love and acceptance into your heart center; exhale the same divine love toward the person you are visualizing. The person can also be you.

Throughout your day...

✳ Be aware of and thankful for kindness and generosity extended to you.

Choose kindness and generosity.

Transforming Fear

The single most empowering thing we can do for ourselves is to transform fear.

While fear contains tremendous power, it doesn't propel us forward and upward but, rather, drags us down and chains us to the past. Freeing ourselves from fear is a loving intention because, as fear subsides, we are better able to access the soft, sweet power of our hearts, which naturally leads to loving ourselves and others more freely and completely.

It's important to realize that we are not our fear—we simply experience it. Please, never accept a definition of yourself that identifies you as your fear. Fear is not something we *are* but something we *have*. For example, you may have told yourself, "I'm such a loser." Although you may feel fearful and defeated at times, that does not mean you're a loser. In fact, any mindful attempt made to transform fear makes you a wise and courageous winner.

The following practice is called disidentification. It is exactly what the name implies: a technique that helps you take a step back and realize that fear (and other emotions or thoughts) are not who you are but something you have and can change. Disidentification can dilute the power of fear.

Practice...

* Think of some sentences that appeal to you as definitions of who you are now or want to become. For example:

> *I am a loving and lovable woman.*

I am a wise and wonderful woman.

I am perfectly okay just as I am at this moment.

✳ When fear arises, pay attention to it, name it, and then repeat several times, "I have a fear of (failure, heights, abandonment, blind dates, and so on), but I am *not* this fear!"

✳ Take a moment to breathe in the fact that you are much more than any fear you have. Exhale any vestiges of the named fear into the atmosphere to be transformed into light and love.

Throughout your day...

✳ Transform fearful energy into positive by affirming what you *are*. Add a sentence of your choosing to the disidentification statement. For instance, I might say, "I have a fear of rejection, but I am not this fear. I am a unique and beautiful daughter of the Divine."

✳ I have a fear of _____, but I am not this fear! I am _____.

Courageous woman
Transforms fearfulness into
Loving energy.

inviting serenity through simplicity

It does not matter whether one paints a picture, writes a poem, or carves a statue, simplicity is the mark of a master hand. —Elise de Wolfe

$\mathcal{S}$implicity is a natural by-product of mindfulness. By concentrating attention on one person, feeling, activity, or thing, we invite extraneous and intrusive mind chatter to fade into the background. What remains is awareness of the moment: the pure and simple experience of life as it evolves moment by precious moment.

Just as mindfulness simplifies our internal environment, it is also useful in simplifying our physical surroundings. Being mindful of items we treasure and use regularly, and noticing those that have become superfluous, can guide our choices about what to keep and what to recycle.

Believe it or not, we can simplify our lives if we choose to, and feel much calmer and more balanced as a result. Truly...

Simple is calming. Simple is satisfying.

Simplifying creates inner and outer space; space invites serenity.

Overloading Evolution

Drs. Rick Hanson and Rick Mendius—whose research on the brain's tendency to emphasize negative experiences over positive ones was mentioned in part 1—believe that our brains have not evolved sufficiently to absorb and process the rapidity of stimulation they are constantly bombarded with in our warp-speed, tech-loving society. Not being androids like *Star Trek: The Next Generation*'s Data, is it any wonder we often feel like fussy two-year-olds in desperate need of a nap?

Hopefully, the following computer-overload analogy shared by my son Brett will help assuage any guilt you may have about simplifying. "As Mom was discussing the fact our brains have not yet evolved to a point that allows them to handle the vast amount of stimuli constantly assaulting our senses, it occurred to me that computers have experienced a similar evolutionary challenge. The neocortex of the brain and the RAM (random-access memory) of a computer act as the organizational processing centers of the brain and computer, respectively. The amount of RAM on a computer determines how fast it can work and how many functions it can do at once.

"The first personal computers were equipped with relatively small amounts of RAM. At that time, with no Internet and limited demands for information processing, those computers worked just fine. With the appearance of the Internet, the borders of information availability were blasted beyond our wildest imagination and existing computers quickly became obsolete. Any attempt to process more than one or two applications at a time either slowed your computer to a crawl or locked it up completely.

"As it was with the computer, so it is with our organic equivalent. The stimulus and information flooding us on a daily basis has reached such epic proportions that our brains simply can't keep up. The more we struggle to keep pace—because that's what the world expects of us—the more our brains strain, slow down, and even lock up. So be gentle with your brain. If you allow it to handle just one thing at a time, with great focus and care, I think you will be relieved and amazed at how well it performs."

Practice...

✳ If you feel overloaded and overwhelmed, relax your body and mind by taking several deep breaths. Appreciate your brain for the wonders it performs each moment.

✳ With love and respect for yourself, let go of unrealistic expectations.

Throughout your day...

✳ Adopt a simple, "byte-sized" approach to learning and life.

Live gently with yourself and your brain.

Moving at Your Own Pace

Because of external demands, you may have lost track of your natural pace, the tempo of living that resonates best with your being. I know my internal Energizer Bunny remained ignorant of my natural pace for decades, and I overdid, over-planned, and overpleased long after it was necessary.

I was shocked a few years ago to discover that my natural pace is much slower than I thought. In fact, I thrive best when limiting outside activities to two per day. At my stage of life, that's doable; during the "kid" years it would have been more difficult. I found my true tempo due to unexpected surgery that forced me to stop completely and then move through the recovery period slowly. To my surprise, I *loved* the unhurried pace. For me, Lily Tomlin was right when she proposed, "For fast-acting relief, try slowing down."

Having been "hog-tied and throw'd on the ground," as they say in parts of my home state, I discovered many bless-ings in feeling *under*whelmed. Less stress, bitchiness, and resentment, and more laughs, relaxation, and naps were a few of them. Undoubtedly, the major blessing was the aware-ness that I'm a medium-paced woman, not the fast-paced one I expected myself to be.

The other day a wonderful young woman from whom I get massages said, "I've got *such* a good story to tell you!" Donia shared that she'd been working too hard and was exhausted and even feeling resentful toward clients. A few days before we spoke, Donia was crying on the way to a client's house because she hadn't made the time to say good-bye to a friend who'd died that day. "And, you know what, Sue?" she said with a knowing grin "I was reaching for a tissue and ran my car into a *brick wall!*"

Donia immediately interpreted the accident as a clear message to stop, find her natural pace, and honor it. Being a mindful woman, Donia immediately adopted an attitude of gratitude *and* promised herself to begin moving at her own pace.

Please be kind to yourself by discovering and honoring your natural rhythm and pace.

Practice...

* Nonjudgmentally, pay attention to feeling overwhelmed. Does it come from doing too much? Trying to *be* too much for too many? Overscheduling? Underresting? No solitude?

* Honor your inner knowing about the perfect, right pace for you.

* When possible, schedule only those activities that elicit a "Yes!" from your heart.

Throughout your day...

* Take time for literal breathers. Pause between tasks, at stoplights, or while waiting for kids, and take several deep, slow breaths. Imagine energy coming into your body and tension flowing out.

Carve out much-needed times of *under*whelm.

Lubricating Life with Time

Author Hugh Prather is one of the nicest, most laid-back men I've met. Yet his writings reveal that he, too, must be mindful in order not to lose his good nature by overcommitting and rushing. He writes, "I notice that when I place myself under a time constraint, when I set a deadline and rush to meet it, it's virtually impossible to keep from outwardly blaming or mentally attacking other people. Yet time can be a lubricant as well as a point of friction. Today I will give myself, my mind, and all that I do more than enough time" (2005, 100).

Being overly familiar with time—or the shortage of it—as a point of friction, I love the concept of time as a lubricant! The picture that popped into my mind while reading about him giving himself more than enough time was that of a small moat surrounding activities, a watery decompression chamber on which to float before moving on to the next thing.

Water is a wonderful symbol of relaxation and rejuvenation to me, but something else may be more calming for you. If you are a nature lover, imagining a few moments in a forest clearing, or actually going outside, might help you catch your breath, depressurize, and prepare for the next thing you want or need to do. Or perhaps simply *deciding* to give yourself more than enough time will make it happen.

Of course, there are women who love being as busy as possible. If you thrive on back-to-back activities or are energized by having a packed scheduled, you are probably one of them. That's great, as long as you're keeping the pace you *want* to, not one that you (or others) feel you *should* maintain. Most of us, however, feel the friction of time pressure at least some of the time and can benefit from simplifying our lives in ways that give us time to truly enjoy all that we do.

We are not, after all, slaves to the schedules we create. With awareness, self-care, and planning, we can lubricate our lives with the stress-reducing pleasure of enough time.

Practice...

✳ Take time to muse about how it would feel to have enough time. Mindfully explore such questions as these: Do I need fewer obligations? Would more time alone be good? How can I create space and time between activities? What can I do to simplify my life in ways that feel self-nurturing?

✳ At least once this week, simplify your life in a way that gives you more than enough time.

✳ If having enough time brings a modicum of serenity, gift yourself by making it a habit.

Throughout your day...

✳ Lubricate your life with a few well-timed free minutes.

Surround tasks and activities with time.

Opting for Simplicity of Thought

Simplicity of thought enhances warmth of heart.

I believe our instinctual nature is to feel great warmth and love toward ourselves, others, and the natural world; to be open to all people and things we encounter. Babies and puppies are good examples of inborn openness. Unless they've learned to be fearful or cautious, babies will smile upon the best and the worst. The same concept is true for puppies. Some very effective puppy training schools are housed in prisons. Inmates do the preliminary socialization and obedience training for service dogs and the dogs unconditionally love their trainers. Many of the inmates involved begin believing in their dogs and end up believing in themselves, perhaps for the first time.

Babies and dogs don't let tangled thoughts overshadow their natural inclination to love and trust. When not mistreated or traumatized, they remain free from mind clutter and, as a result, are able to spread great warmth and love in their wake. With a bit of mindful decluttering, so can you.

How and what we think is one of the few things over which we have control. Prem Rawat, also known as Maharaji, a very appealing teacher on inner peace since the age of eight, says, "The gift of thinking is one of the greatest gifts that God has given you, but what you think *about* is your gift to yourself." I know it's possible to give yourself the gift of simple, positive thinking because I retrained myself to do it. My mother was a wonderful woman, but she was bedeviled by worry much of the time. And I was an apt apprentice.

I use the following techniques to simplify both my inner and outer lives. At first glance they may seem too simplistic to work, but they are powerful tools. The scope of *The Mindful Woman* requires brevity. If you'd like to pursue these methods in depth, please see my book *The Courage to Be Yourself.*

Practice...

✳ Pick a simple, positive statement and repeat it to override turbulent thoughts and worries. Two of my sentences are "I can do all things through God, who strengthens me" and "I am a lovable and good woman even though I make mistakes."

✳ Adopt the KISS (**K**eep **I**t **S**imple, **S**weetie) philosophy by mindfully simplifying and sweetening your thoughts.

Throughout your day...

✳ Simply love yourself.

Simple thoughts invite a quiet mind and warm heart.

Being For, Not Against

It takes a lot of energy to get riled up over anything—politics, the state of our country's schools, health care, our own health, real or imagined slights from friends or mates, and whatever maddens you personally. Not only do we expend an exorbitant amount of energy getting riled up, it also leads to overproduction of bile by the liver, which hinders rather than helps digestion and can lead to gallstones among other ailments. Being chronically worried and upset promotes emotional discomfort and physical disease.

I was touched by a squib in *USA Today* recently. ESPN's Peter Gammons shared that following his recovery from a brain aneurysm, the same thing that killed his sister eleven years earlier, he doesn't worry much anymore. He said, "You know what it's like on talk radio, how people get so upset? Well, now I'm focused on what I'm *for*, not what I'm against. That's sort of my new life motto, 'What I'm for.'" How wonderfully simple.

I noticed Mr. Gammon decided to *focus* on what he's for, not against. While he might not word it this way, he's become more mindful of where he puts his attention.

I don't think anyone would disagree that there is much in the world that needs changing, but what if we changed our attitude toward it? Instead of being *against* the way schools are run, let's be *for* children getting the best education and vote accordingly, volunteer in the classroom, and see that teachers get the salaries they deserve. For those of us aghast at the thought of war and the pain it visits on so many, we can be *for* peace. And we can be *for* those whose lives have been torn apart by war and do what we can to ease their pain. For example, we can write the wounded and our congresspersons, donate to good causes, reach out to widows and their children, or visit hospitals.

Being for something creates an upswing of energy and love that being against does not. Being for empowers and lightens, being against depletes and darkens. Being for is openhearted and embracing.

Practice...

✳ If you become aware of feeling or speaking against something, pause. If it's safe, softly close your eyes and take two deep breaths. Direct your next three breaths to your heart.

✳ Ask yourself, "What can I be *for* in this?"

Throughout your day...

✳ Focus on what you're *for*.

**Being *for* brightens your day
and lightens your heart.**

Discovering Simple Solutions

There are hundreds of simple solutions to many of life's annoyances, but often they seem to hover just outside our awareness, waiting for us to discover them. And discover them we must, because small irritants can become the equivalent of Chinese water torture, drip, drip, dripping on our psyches until we are worn down and tired out. Traffic is a personal torture of mine. After battling the noontime traffic downtown and almost being hit by a bus a few days ago, I felt as if my teeth were ground down a quarter of an inch. It was a good *re*learning because I was impatient and wanted to do my errand *now* and, as a result, broke my simple-solution rule of not being caught downtown during high-traffic times.

By bringing your attention to the here and now and listening to your own wisdom, it's possible to come up with many simple solutions for things that aggravate you. It's overscheduled impatience that often renders us—at least, *me*—deaf to our own perceptions. For your own sanity, try an experiment: When an annoying situation arises, give yourself a time-out. Consciously bring your awareness into the moment. Loosen your jaw, pay attention to several breaths, and then take a deep breath and let it out with an exaggerated sigh. Sigh again, deeply and loudly. I used to cringe when my mother sighed, but I now believe she was wisely releasing energy.

Having relaxed a bit by sighing, smile and ask yourself, "What's a simple solution here?"

While I know there are innumerable times when simple solutions are not enough, often simplicity can bring the relief and resolution needed. Remember that no matter what the circumstances, we have the power to simplify our responses to them and our thoughts about them.

Practice...

Following are a few samples of simple solutions. You will create different ones to meet your personal needs.

Annoyance	Simple Solution
Whining child	Give five minutes of UDA (undivided attention)
Being asked to do something you don't want to do	Say no nicely but firmly.
Feeling tense	Relax your jaw and breathe in through your nose and out through your mouth
Loud movie or concert	Wear earplugs
Exhaustion	Take a walk or short nap
Need to vent	Talk to a *trusted* woman friend.

Throughout your day...

✳ Discover a simple solution whenever possible.

Invite serenity by trying simplicity first.

Rightsizing Each Day

Whopper sandwiches, whopper schedules, and whopper lives seem to be the trend. If you are a natural-born whopper who thrives on lots of stimulation and nonstop doing, then you are in your element. But, if you're a highly sensitive woman or simply more laid-back, trying to manage one whopper day after another is probably not a balanced existence for you.

A cluttered physical space and an overcrowded calendar can translate into confused thoughts and feelings. Stuff takes up space, both literally and energetically. Removing extraneous items from your physical space frees up emotional and mental room as well. Mindfulness is more likely to flourish when surrounded by inner and outer space. Becoming aware of your unique tolerance levels helps you rightsize the stuff you have and the stuff you do.

In her book *Rightsizing Your Life*, author Ciji Ware makes an interesting point: "People need to be mindful of what's going on in their lives *now*. Rightsizing is a process, not an event, and its outcome has more to do with the 'right' of the equation than the 'size'" (2007, 4). I resonate with the idea of rightsizing being an ongoing process and that "right" is the operative word. What is right for you may not be right for me. Because life is the ultimate process, what is right for you at this point in time will, undoubtedly, change as circumstances do. For instance, if you have children at home, lots of animals to care for, or work eighty hours a week, you have much different needs now than you may later. The important question is what is the rightsized day for you *now*?

Practice...

✳ Calm and quiet your body, mind, and spirit. Use a
   technique that appeals to you now.

✳ From a calm center, imagine a perfectly sized day.
   Is such a day possible more often than not?

✳ If rightsizing is impossible now, how can you
   "better-size" in order to become calm and
   balanced? For your mental and emotional welfare,
   please try to better-size at least three days a week.

✳ Really *see* the stuff you've accumulated. Keep only
   what you love or need.

Throughout your day...

✳ Recycle, donate, or throw away something that
   hasn't been used in two years.

✳ Drop all that isn't necessary or much loved.

**A rightsized day has time and space for
laughter, love, and listening.**

Expecting the Best

Even if you learned to worry or expect the worst while growing up, you have the power and maturity to change those negative and stressful habits as an adult. Because fears and limiting expectations arise from recurrent patterns of behavior imprinted through frequent repetition, mindfulness helps you notice and alter patterns that are no longer working for you. Choosing to change a worry-prone mind-set, and paying attention when worry engulfs you, empowers you to transform knee-jerk responses and automatic attitudes.

As we explored earlier, our brains are wired to focus on fearful and negative stimuli, so please don't be hard on yourself if you tend to worry and look on the dark side. But please *do* free yourself from the habit. There is nothing simple or serene about either worry or a fearful inclination to expect the worst. Both suck up tremendous amounts of psychic and emotional energy and waste vast quantities of time. My dad used to joke about worry by saying, "Don't tell me worrying doesn't work. Most of the things I worry about never happen!" He was right. Many of the things we worry and fret about either resolve themselves or never materialize at all.

A mind preoccupied with worry and fear is unable to perceive the good, loving, and beautiful. Worry and fear block the light as surely as dark clouds block the sun. Responding to the law of attraction, worry and fear draw more of the same toward us. Thankfully, the opposite is also true: gratitude, calmness, and courage attract similar energies. By intentionally adopting a positive attitude, expecting the best, and replacing worry with gratitude, beneficial energy and desired outcomes will be drawn to us more often than not.

Practice...

* Energy follows intention and attention. Therefore, when you become aware of worrying, set an intention to choose gratitude instead. Draw your attention to three things or people for which you feel grateful. Dwell on the reasons you are thankful for and appreciative of them.

* Express sincere, personalized gratitude to at least one person each day.

* Even if it feels contrived, imagine the best possible outcome for a stressful or hurtful situation. Embellish your fantasy outcome, and enjoy it to the fullest.

* Keep practicing until you have a habit of expecting the best. Until that happens, contrived optimism is better than no optimism at all.

Throughout your day...

* Choose gratitude and expect the best.

Expecting the best attracts the best; gratitude takes care of the rest.

Noticing Singular Beauty

Perched atop a rock outcropping stands a single cypress tree that has become a well-known symbol of the California coastline. For over two hundred and fifty years, the Lone Cypress has inspired artists, photographers, tourists, and residents who travel 17 Mile Drive between Pacific Grove and Carmel. What is it about this small tree that makes me and countless others want to stay in its presence for as long as we can?

As I try to find the words to describe my response to the Lone Cypress, none seem adequate. However, my mind conjures up memories of the last time I saw the tree, and my eyes fill with tears. The Pacific Ocean was by no means passive and tranquil that day; winds howled and huge waves surged against the Lone Cypress's rock home. Although my windbreaker was no match for the storm, I stayed put, admiring the cypress's tenacity and strength in the face of the lashing it was taking.

Perhaps I was mesmerized because the cypress stands alone, unvanquished by either the frantic wind or the turbulent sea. A singular object of beauty silhouetted against the ever-changing backdrop of the vast, mysterious ocean. A symbol of survival and inspiration. Whatever the reason, I returned to our motel room drenched in awe as well as water.

It strikes me that each of us has something in common with the Lone Cypress. We are battered by storms, stand firm on rocky ground, become symbols of courage by surviving hardship with grace, and bring our own matchless beauty and inspiration to the world. Without egotism or conceit, we need to accept our own excellence. Recognizing the love, joy, compassion, and beauty you have to offer helps you accept the sacred responsibility for sharing it. As a single cypress inspired me, *you* can inspire others.

Practice...

✳ Each day, be aware of at least one example of singular beauty. Allow it to inspire you.

✳ Quietly pay attention to your breath as it flows naturally to and from your body.

✳ From a calm, centered state, invite your unique qualities of beauty and excellence to say hello. Without emotional attachment, make a list of attributes and attitudes that can bring more light, love, and joy to people and the planet.

✳ Feel gratitude for these qualities.

Throughout your day...

✳ Allow your singular beauty to be a blessing.

**Generously share
Your beauty and excellence
Openheartedly.**

chapter 9

fulfilling the promise
of presence

You, yourself, as much as anybody in the entire universe, deserve your love and affection. —Buddha

How to fulfill the promise of presence can be illustrated by the familiar story about a young woman who stopped a wise man on the streets of New York and asked, "Do you know the way to Carnegie Hall?" The man replied, "Practice, practice, practice."

While presence enriches our lives immeasurably, most promises of presence are not fulfilled immediately but unfold as a result of desire, intention, and, yes, practice. In this chapter, we will explore some of the many possibilities available when we are fully present to ourselves and our lives. Among them are joy, trust, wholeness, strength, love of body, and alignment with God/good.

True presence increases love and compassion. As the Buddha said, no one deserves your love and affection more than you do. Being nonjudgmentally present to yourself gives you the opportunity to fully understand, enjoy, and appreciate the unique being you are. As a result of enjoying a deep, spiritually based love and appreciation for yourself, an ever-flowing wellspring of love is created within you. From this fountainhead, compassion and caring flow freely and easily toward other beings. Because of its subsequent outflow, I believe self-love is one of the highest callings we can answer.

Simply by being attentively and openheartedly present—whether to yourself, work, family, others, or a cause—more love is added to the fabric of life, and *love is the answer, no matter what the question.*

Awakening Beginner's Mind

If you've ever taken a walk with an inquisitive two-year-old or an especially olfactory-endowed dog, you know what "beginner's mind" (or, in the case of our dog, Lily, "beginner's nose") is like. Everything is worth exploring—each flower, bug, and distraction worth full attention. No matter how often Lily and I travel the same path, she is the epitome of focus and concentration on each and every scent that attracts her attention *this* time. Because she's absolutely present to the experience of the moment, Lily's become my guru of outdoor beginner's-mind practice.

Beginners themselves, children are great teachers of beginner's mind. A healthy child looks at the world with excitement and takes time to be truly present to all offerings. Thankfully, most young children have the luxury of enough time to naturally pursue their affinity for beginner's mind. You, as a busy woman, will need to consciously create an intention toward beginner's mind and make the time to perceive with a fresh outlook.

When approached with beginner's mind, a few moments can turn into what my friend Jean calls "an indelible ten minutes." Driving alone from Colorado to Iowa, Jean took a break at a rest stop in Nebraska. Instead of hurriedly eating her lunch and hopping back in the car, Jean paused to enjoy this particular view of her home state. To her surprise, she found the vista absolutely stunning.

With tears on her lashes, she told me, "I was amazed to be so moved. I even said aloud, 'This is home,' and tears rolled down my cheeks." She went on to explain, "Words can't really describe the feelings of awe and mystery that filled those ten indelible minutes of my life."

The Mindful Woman was written around the central theme of "a few mindful moments make a world of difference." The thought of constant mindfulness was too grandiose for me to grasp at this point in my evolution. But a few moments each day? Yes, I can do that. As each of us practices and reaps the benefits of conscious presence, I absolutely believe moments will naturally expand into a more mindful life.

Practice...

✳ With openness and kind curiosity, be totally present to a person, thing, or experience at least twice a day.

Throughout your day...

✳ Consciously look, listen, and learn with childlike enthusiasm.

A few moments of beginner's mind make a world of difference.

In-Bodying Life

Purposefully living *in* your body and paying loving and tender attention to it on a regular basis is not only helpful to your magnificent physical self but is also one of the most effective ways to restore balance and calm to your emotions, mind, and spirit. Although it's easy to ignore our bodies and take them for granted unless they call attention to themselves by breaking down or functioning poorly, it is unwise to do so. The body is one part of the four quadrants of your being: physical, emotional, mental, and spiritual. Neglecting the body is akin to sawing one leg off a four-legged stool. Equilibrium, strength, and balance are achieved through respect for and attention to emotions, mind, spirit, *and* body.

While a few exercise programs still tout the idea of "no pain, no gain," there are innumerable programs and practices that honor body-wisdom while strengthening your body. Yoga is one.

I have known Julie, a brilliant, incredibly creative, and formerly intense publisher, for over twenty years. "Brilliant" and "creative" are still excellent words to describe her, but "intense" no longer fits. What changed? She's practicing yoga. Because the practice of yoga has made such a noticeable difference in Julie's life and attitude, I asked her to share a little of her experience with you.

She writes, "Gentle yoga has changed my life. In only two one-and-one-half-hour sessions a week, yoga enables me to completely step outside my very busy, stressful, and sometimes chaotic life to clear my mind and feel and appreciate my whole body." For those of us who have body issues—and who among us doesn't?—Julie's next comments are especially encouraging: "Yoga has calmed by mind and made me much more aware and respectful of my body. I love my body now and am so thankful it has served me well all these years."

While yoga may not be your path to living in and loving your body, please give yourself the gift of finding some form of stretching or exercise that does help you relax and strengthen your body, soothe and transform your emotions, calm and quiet your mind, and restore your spirit.

Practice...

✳ Remembering that breath is the bridge between body and mind, with respectful awareness, gently breathe into various parts of your body—especially those that are uncomfortable. Thank them for all they have done and will do for you.

✳ Move. Stretch. Restore and energize your body lovingly and appreciatively.

Throughout your day...

✳ With great respect, pay attention to your body, emotions, mind, and spirit.

Bridge body and mind with breath.

Perceiving Wholeness

A peach tree, plus all the fruit it will ever yield, is present in the original seed. The same is true of us. As newborns, we are whole, brimming with everything required for growth, learning, loving, having fun, and being authentic. Wholeness is still within us as adults; some aspects of it are realized, while others wait their turn for potential to mature into reality.

Even though we have everything we need within us, it's important to remember that we are also always in some phase of beginningness. Consistently uncovering yet another inner treasure—or termite—is the nature of evolution and growth. Good ways to facilitate perceiving wholeness within you are to be gentle and kind to the tender shoots of your beginnings, to trust the process of moving from one awareness to the next, and to have patience with each step and stumble along the way. Accepting yourself as is, while compassionately aspiring to feel and express more of your inborn wholeness, is an attainable promise of presence.

Being present and truly listening to your soul's song allows you to know yourself deeply, to become acquainted with your larger, spirit-self as well as the small-self each of us has acquired through trial, error, and injury. Turning within and tuning in to your loving and complete spirit-self gradually but surely instills a growing perception of your innate wholeness and goodness into your mind and feelings.

A quiet, present mind absorbs insights and inspiration from the Divine, whose whispers become your thoughts and, in turn, are reflected in your life and loves. In the sunny warmth of attention and presence, wholeness can organically reveal itself one precious awareness at a time.

Practice...

✳ After a few centering and calming breaths, breathe in the affirmation "I am whole and good." Inhale "I am..." Exhale "...whole and good."

✳ Relax into affirming whatever comes into your mind effortlessly; for instance, "I am ... well." "I am ... loving." "I am ... wise."

✳ Return to "I am ... whole and good" for several breaths.

✳ Invite into your mind's eye a symbol or visual image of yourself radiating wholeness.

✳ Rest in the certainty that wholeness is a priceless inheritance from the Divine.

Throughout your day...

✳ Remind yourself that you are whole, authentic, and good.

✳ Tap into your superb spirit-self and feel, speak, and act from her point of view.

You are simply peachy in God's eyes.

Instilling Strength

Many fears and weaknesses hang around because we try to ignore them, overpower them, or outthink them. This doesn't work. Relegated to the unconscious mind, fears and weaknesses grow in power and potency. However, meeting our demons in the light of nonjudgmental stillness encourages them to transform into strength and empowerment.

Willingly greeting our fears and weaknesses with openness, acceptance, and respect is one of the hardest tasks mindfulness asks of us and one of the most freeing practices we can undertake. Sitting in stillness with our sorrow and shame, our fear and judgment laid bare is an act of courage.

The demon I'm sitting with right now is judgment of another person, which spawns judgment of myself laced with guilt and shame for being a "bad" woman. Only recently have I had enough self-love to *really* look at and accept this judgment-weakness with the goal of transforming it into strength.

As often happens when we're on a path to improved mindfulness, the perfect teacher has appeared for me. I've developed an aversion to a person with whom I attend a class once a week. I have a fantasy that my beloved mother, whose deathbed confession was that her main fault was judgment, has arranged this opportunity for me.

Mindfulness accepts experience and allows it to be our teacher. To let this experience teach me, I am being present to my tight jaws and constricted chest whenever I see or think about the person. I bring my attention back to my breath and relax into the feelings of the moment.

Yesterday, I felt a tiny glimmer of what the future might bring. Upon seeing my "teacher," I smiled at how creatively and speedily judgment leapt into my mind and agitated my body and emotions. Viewed with a touch of amusement, the difficult feelings dissipated quickly, which gave me hope and helped me trust the Buddha's assurance that "mindfulness is all-helpful."

Practice...

✳ Sit in stillness for a few minutes with no agenda.

✳ Continue sitting in stillness. If demons surface, bless them and let them go.

✳ Breathe in "I am..." Breathe out "...strong."

Throughout your day...

✳ Greet your feelings with gentle acceptance.

Strength reveals itself in stillness.

The Healing Power of Listening

Early in my counseling career, I realized many of my clients' yearnings could be encapsulated into three simple desires: See me. Hear me. Hold me. Undivided attention grants others their wishes to be seen, heard, and held—held in arms or held in hearts and awareness. Attentive listening allows God to work through us. Mindfulness practice is instrumental in creating within you the unhurried calmness, emotional balance, and openheartedness it takes to truly listen.

If you've known a gifted listener, you've probably experienced coming away from their presence feeling validated, uplifted, comforted, and perhaps even blessed with a healing insight or awareness. My friend Virginia is a listener extraordinaire. Although she rarely gives advice, Virginia listens so attentively that it's not unusual for her to pinpoint exactly what is keeping the talker from feeling better, getting unstuck, or making healthier choices. Without ego—or names—she shared that she had recently had lunch with three women, and each had gone away having made a decision that had been nagging at her for weeks. "After hearing their dilemmas," she explained excitedly, "it just seemed so obvious what they wanted or needed to do. I asked a question or two and they *knew*. It was fun."

It's also fun to listen to ourselves. Well, maybe it's not always *fun*, but it is essential that we listen to ourselves as completely and compassionately as we do others. How else will we know who we authentically are, what we're experiencing in the moment, and what path we'd like to take next? Listening to ourselves can be both healing and enlightening.

In his lovely book *Morning Notes*, Hugh Prather writes, "We do our best when we don't try to go it alone. Instead, we take God's hand and above all we take God's advice, which can be heard by anyone who just stops a moment and is still" (2005, iii). Going it alone may not mean God is the only one left out of the equation. We can also leave ourselves out if we don't pause to truly listen to what our hearts and minds are trying to tell us. Mindfulness helps us form loving partnerships with ourselves and God.

Practice...

❉ Quietly sit for a few moments and follow the inflow and outflow of your breath.

❉ Effortlessly, *listen to* what your mind and heart are expressing right now.

❉ Effortlessly, hold your inner self in the ways she yearns to be held.

❉ Take God's hand as you return to your breath for a few more minutes.

Throughout your day...

❉ Lay aside any agenda you may have and truly listen to two people for a few minutes each.

We express love through listening.

Seeing Synchronicity

During a meditation-class exercise, we went outside to mindfully notice whatever caught our eye. I was also asking for angels to be with a friend's daughter who was hovering near death. After praying, I glanced at the sky and was delighted to see a huge cloud shaped exactly as I imagine an angel wing might look. The cloud felt like an angelic nod, an assurance. My heart lifted with hope. Although she still has health challenges, my friend's daughter did survive.

At the opposite end of the spectrum, the teacher of the class noticed how the trash was spilling artistically from the trash barrel. He'd never before realized how colorful trash could be and returned to class filled with joy and gratitude that he could perceive color. I had actually observed his trash watching with a chuckle and was able to relate to what he'd seen. It *was* pretty. "Coincidentally," a class member whose feelings of dread about upcoming eye surgery had kept her from noticing anything during the exercise, related that our stories had turned her mind from fear toward gratitude. A pretty good miracle in itself.

Experiencing joy as a result of noticing both the ethereal and the earthy within a few mindful minutes helped me realize there must be synchronistic miracles available in every moment. We simply need to be present and awake enough to see them.

On the first anniversary of her husband's death, a friend tearfully reported that she had fully awakened at 3:48 AM, the exact minute he had died the previous year. Since she had never awakened at that time before, she took it as a loving "wake-up call" from her husband and felt sadly joyful and deeply comforted by it.

Synchronicities, such as the angel wing cloud following my prayer and my friend's early morning visit, make me feel *heard*. They deepen my belief that God, angels, loved ones, and other celestial emissaries are available and completely in love with us. The wonderful Sufi saying "God is the Beloved who kisses us on the inside of our hearts" rings resoundingly true in the face of sweet synchronicities.

Practice...

* Instead of brushing aside or barely noticing synchronicities, rest in the wonder of them.

* See synchronicities and coincidences as possible miniature and major miracles.

Throughout your day...

* Embrace the idea of being kissed on the inside of your heart by the Beloved.

**It's fun to see synchronicity
as divine instant messaging.**

Trusting in Goodness

Because trust is a huge issue for many women, I am aware that trusting in goodness may be a hard idea to swallow. But since trust is an effective antidote for fear and insecurity, we need to trust—especially in goodness—no matter how many times we've been betrayed, wounded, or let down. Yes, there is tremendous darkness in the world, and man's inhumanity to man can break our hearts. However, we don't bring more humanity, light, and compassion into the world by concentrating on their opposites. The way to bring more good into being is to do what we can to alleviate the darkness and add light by the way we live our own lives.

An excellent way to cultivate trust in God and goodness is to recognize and act from the goodness that is within us right now, this very moment, even though we are all imperfect and still a work in progress. One of the best messages I ever received from a sermon was in the form of a little button that read "PBPWMGIFWMY" and stood for "Please be patient with me; God isn't finished with me yet." No matter where you are in your evolution, you undoubtedly have more goodness in your heart than you are aware of.

To augment the ability to trust, it's important to remember that energy flows where attention goes. By focusing your awareness and attention on the goodness in and around you, positive energy flows toward it and goodness multiplies. The more goodness you become aware of and express, the easier it is to naturally trust in goodness itself. Surely seeing and creating goodness is a sacred calling.

Practice...

✳ Sit quietly and relax into the rhythm of your breath and heartbeat.

✳ As you inhale, invite the soothing goodness of God to flow effortlessly into your body, mind, emotions, and spirit. As you exhale, send out goodwill and positive thoughts to whomever or whatever floats into your awareness.

✳ Use the power of prayer for others. Send wishes for happiness and peace of mind to someone.

Throughout your day...

✳ Accentuate the positive by focusing on goodness.

✳ Consciously do three good deeds daily.

I inhale great draughts of space,
The east and west are mine,
and the north and south are mine.
I am larger, better than I thought,
I did not know I held so much goodness.
—Walt Whitman, "Song of the Road"

Doing unto Others

Because it expresses ageless wisdom regarding living a good life, the Golden Rule is taught across the world's religions. Here are some examples:

Christianity: In everything, do to others as you would have them do to you. (Jesus)

Buddhism: Treat not others in ways that you yourself would find hurtful. (Buddha)

Judaism: What is hateful to you, do not do to your neighbor. This is the whole Torah; all the rest is commentary. Go and learn it. (Hillel)

Hinduism: Do not do to others what would cause pain if done to you. (Mahábhárata)

Islam: Not one of you truly believes until you wish for others what you wish for yourself. (The Prophet Muhammad)

Sufism: The basis of Sufism is consideration of the hearts and feelings of others. If you haven't the will to gladden someone's heart, then at least beware lest you hurt someone's heart, for that is our path. (Dr. Javad Nurbakhsh)

Native American Spirituality: All things are our relatives; what we do to everything, we do to ourselves. (Black Elk)

Living the Golden Rule philosophy is easier when you are present to other beings, the earth, yourself, and the moment. Conscious, aware presence to anything deepens our understanding of it. Understanding opens our hearts. Acting from the center of our hearts promotes both personal and global peace. Practiced faithfully, the Golden Rule is the only guideline we need for leading a compassionately mindful life.

Practice...

* Choose your favorite version of the Golden Rule and put it in a place where you can see it often. My friend Amanda's reminder is worded humorously: "If it ain't nice, don't say it or do it!"

* Treat all beings with compassion and respect.

* Walk with gentle feet upon your Mother Earth.

Throughout your day...

* Hold each heart, including your own, in the softest of embraces.

Do unto others...

Highlighting Loving-Kindness

Among many possible definitions for "loving-kindness" are goodwill, compassion, consideration, understanding, and concern for the well-being of ourselves and others. Loving-kindness is a natural outcome of openheartedness, which is greatly enhanced by the practice of mindful presence.

Highlighting loving-kindness means consciously *choosing* to be, feel, and act kind and loving in any given moment. To help remind her to choose loving-kindness, Lenni, a client, pauses to ask herself the question "What is loving right now in the current situation?" Lenni told me that getting the answer is not difficult, but *feeling* loving can be tough. "Sometimes, I just say 'yeah, right' and continue to feel anything but loving and kind. However, I've been asking the question long enough that I rarely consciously *act* unloving or unkind."

Because we are human, we will not always choose loving-kindness, but since spiritual teachers and sages have taught for eons that our true nature is love, reflecting loving-kindness helps align us with our innate authenticity and our higher selves. Expressing the integrity of your highest self is one of the best ways to find peace of mind and generate a sense of joy and purpose.

Being compassionately present in the moment and consistently practicing loving-kindness allows you to bring light into shadow and comfort into sorrow. Generously sharing the priceless blessing of loving-kindness with yourself, others, and the world sends ripples of compassion and caring farther, wider, and deeper than you can ever imagine.

Light dispels darkness. Love is an attitude of light, and kindness is light in action. Therefore, fulfilling the promise of presence and performing conscious acts of loving-kindness makes us invaluable light bearers in a time when darkness shrouds so many people and places.

May we increase light upon our precious planet by intentionally practicing loving-kindness each moment we can.

Practice...

✳ Please remember that the practice of loving-kindness begins with self and, from that openhearted center, extends to others.

✳ Spread light by being kind and loving.

Throughout your day...

✳ Consciously choose loving-kindness.

**The gift of presence
Promises loving-kindness
Is available.**

part three

enjoying the benefits

chapter 10

why mindfulness
feels so good

Mindfulness doesn't cure all, but it always cures.
It corrects the mind's natural tendency toward
dispersion, diffusion, and agitation, redeploying
mental energy toward insight, clarity, and well-being.
—Thich Nhat Hanh

few minutes of mindfulness can make a world of difference in how you feel and act. Even if you're thrashing around in the oblivion of distraction and obligation, simply paying attention to your breath grounds you in the here and now and, as a result, brings you closer to balance, harmony, and awareness. As the bridge between body and mind, breath leads us home to our bodies when we've wandered far afield via such avenues as busyness, frustration, anxiety, or preoccupation.

Agitation and feeling overwhelmed can drop your energy levels so low that your zest for life is diminished. Practicing mindfulness is calming and centering and, therefore, adds to your energy storehouse. An abundance of energy enlivens you, giving you the oomph to be more engaged with yourself, others, and life in general. Mindfulness encourages energized inner and outer connections.

Along with increased energy, mindfulness promotes inner spaciousness, clarity, and well-being. While automatic behaviors and fear-driven feelings *contract* our lives and cause us to hover in an atmosphere of limitation generated by our small-selves, mindfully being present to our actions, reactions, and choices is incredibly *expansive*. In the spaciousness of expansion and peace of mind, our calm, wise, and intuitive self is able to fully function. Expansion and spaciousness open our hearts, allowing us to hear the sweet whispers of spirit.

Awareness First

Mindfulness leads to awareness. Awareness is the first step on the path to change. With awareness, you gain insight into the facets of your life that need balance, the parts of yourself that yearn for calm, and the times and situations in which your heart is tempted to close. With commitment, important insights can lead to equally important actions that improve your life exponentially. Bringing an intentional and nonjudgmental awareness to yourself and your environment opens your mind and heart to the best choices available. Such awareness empowers you to make wise, healthy, and mature choices based on real and appropriate needs and desires. Conscious choice is freedom.

With greater awareness of yourself, you can appreciate what is working for you and alter what isn't in gentle, supportive ways. Awareness helps you take responsibility for your personal life and be accountable for your actions and experiences. Awareness and maturity dance hand in hand. Maturity is not the overresponsible, drudgery-inducing ball and chain that perpetual Peter Pans would have us believe. Maturity is a freeing state of being that gleefully waves good-bye to any victim persona lurking within and consistently acts in ways that help create a joyful, productive, fun, and purposeful life. Awareness built through the practice of mindfulness helps us mature in loving, light, and laugh-filled ways.

As with most everything, maturity is an ongoing process, and we are never too old to learn new things that make mindfulness and joy more possible. As an example, neither I nor my husband, Gene, could be considered spring chickens, but we recently committed to giving up complaining, criticizing, and gossiping by wearing the purple Complaint-Free World bracelets written about in chapter 5 in the section called "Giving Up Grumbling." Even though we weren't big on complaining, criticizing, and gossiping before making the commitment, both of us feel happier as a result of wearing the bracelets because they increase our awareness of the temptation to indulge in any habit that dampens good feelings.

Truth be told, I can benefit from the reminders more than Gene, but he did have a funny experience with it. Because his golf game had been iffy for several outings and he didn't want the bracelet to be a distraction—both physically and mentally, I suspect—he decided not to wear it the next time he went out to play. After the round, he laughingly told me, "Even though I didn't have the bracelet on, I could *feel* it on my wrist!" He also had more fun and no angst at all, even when shots were less accurate than he'd hoped.

Besides feeling lighter and happier since wearing the bracelet, I've experienced an unanticipated side effect. I've stopped swearing. For decades I've believed that using my few favorite swear words was pretty benign and simply added "flavor" to my personality. Interestingly, in monitoring my responses and reactions due to the purple bracelet, I became aware that swearing insidiously exacerbated negative emotions, no matter how seemingly innocuous the words I chose. Although I didn't set out to stop swearing, it simply happened as a result of increased awareness. Surprisingly, I don't miss it at all. Go figure … Visit AComplaintFreeWorld.org if you are interested in learning more.

Another incredibly important awareness to cultivate is knowing how tired you are. Tiredness dulls positive feelings and experiences and intensifies negative ones. My wonderful mother, who was often overworked and underappreciated, had a little sign in her kitchen window stating, "Dearie is Weary." As an adult, I wish I'd paid more attention to that obvious plea for a little help lightening the load. But, as a kid, I simply chuckled and chalked it up as one more of Mother's idiosyncrasies. If you have a similar sign hanging in a corner of your body or soul, please pay attention to it! In fact, if you get nothing more from practicing mindfulness than the awareness you are tired and need to slow down, and then *do so* regularly, it can dramatically increase your sense of well-being and zest for life.

Although we may get a chuckle of recognition from Garrison Keillor's claim "I believe in looking reality straight in the eye and denying it," in order to really wake up to the glory of our lives, it's best if we act on Thich Nhat Hanh's belief that "each thought, each action in the sunlight of awareness becomes sacred." Awareness is a priceless and life-enhancing benefit to be gleaned from the practice of mindfulness.

Freedoms That Follow

Of course the freedoms you gain from mindfulness will be uniquely your own, but I want to underscore a few that I know many women have come to enjoy.

Letting Go

Before I began meditating and consciously practicing mindfulness, letting go was an elusive concept to grasp. In fact, I was particularly good at grasping but not at all adept at letting go. Through increased mindfulness, I am so much better at letting go that I often enjoy the wonderful freedom of being able to release attitudes, actions, expectations, and activities that constrict my life and heart rather than open them.

To me, the first stanza of Reinhold Neibuhr's Serenity Prayer, as adapted by Alcoholics Anonymous, is a beautiful summation of letting go. It is "God, grant me the serenity to accept the things I cannot change; courage to change the things I can; and wisdom to know the difference." With mindfulness, our innate gifts for acceptance, courage, and wisdom are more easily accessible, and letting go becomes possible.

Fundamentally, the best thing we can let go of is the illusion of control in this world of constant change. Yes, there are things we can change and control, but there are also many more people, events, outcomes, and viewpoints over which we have no control beyond that of visualizing and praying for positive resolutions. Holding on to that which we cannot control binds us in fear and resistance.

Jack Kornfield, cofounder of the Insight Meditation Society, refers to the ability to let go as "the wisdom of insecurity" and explains it as "the ability to flow with the changes, to see everything as a process of change, to relax with uncertainty" (Baraz 2007). Elaborating on the idea of letting go, he says, "Meditation [and I believe we can safely add 'mindfulness'] teaches us how to let go, how to stay centered in the midst of change. Once we see that everything is impermanent and ungraspable and that we create a huge amount of suffering if we are attached to things staying the same, we realize that relaxing and letting go is a wiser way to live. Letting go does not mean not caring about things. It means caring for them in a flexible and wise way."

Please be kind to yourself as you move toward the ability to let go. While it's relatively easy to understand the wisdom of letting go, *doing* so is often difficult, especially with those we love the most and to whom we are tightly attached.

My friend Sophie is in the throes of letting go of many familiar patterns—self-blame and excessive worry to name only two—as her married daughter struggles in a difficult and demeaning marriage. "One of the reasons it's so hard," Sophie says, "is that it's like watching myself all over again." After countless sleepless nights and several heartfelt talks with her daughter, Sophie has concluded that she needs to stop believing she can control her daughter and grandchildren's future in any way and simply love them all no matter what happens. "For my own peace of mind, I have to stop blaming myself, put a little distance between myself and the situation, and just love them, love them, love them," she told me recently.

In order to help with the process of letting go, Sophie reminds herself that she did the best she could as a mother and young wife, pulls her thoughts back to the moment when she drifts into fearful what-ifs, sees the beauty and wonder in front of her right now, and is available when her daughter and grandchildren need her. Slowly—it's especially difficult to let go when our children are in pain—Sophie is beginning to sleep better and trust that her daughter will be okay no matter what the outcome.

As Sophie's story illustrates, the more mindfully present we are to what *is*, the less attached we become to our idea of what *should be*. Calmly and nonjudgmentally paying attention to what is—even if it's painful and difficult—keeps us from falling into what I call "the future hole of fear" or being locked in a prison of the past, where regret and recrimination may linger. Although it's becoming almost a cliché, the mindful awareness received from living in the moment and staying in the here and now continues to be a viable and valuable path to greater freedom.

Nonattachment

Nonattachment is a fraternal twin to letting go. Being able to incorporate both letting go and nonattachment into daily life is conducive to emotional balance and peace of mind. In fact, the Buddha taught that the highest happiness comes from "a mind that clings to naught."

For many years, I had the mistaken idea that it was more loving to be absolutely attached to the outcome of all circumstances—my own and other people's—and that feeling others' pain and confusion almost as deeply as they did meant that I really cared. I know I was taught differently during psychotherapy training, but old patterns persisted and I started private practice doing the same overattached, grasping behavior with clients that I had done in my personal life. It took an illness bred of exhaustion and frustration to show me that my attachment had landed me in the same emotional pit my clients inhabited.

Nonattachment does not mean disconnectedness or noncaring. When able to be compassionately detached, we actually feel *more* engaged with and connected to ourselves and other people. Letting go of attachment, especially attachment to a specific outcome, minimizes resistance to our own struggles and, very importantly, frees us from the persistent belief that we must somehow "make it all better" for everyone else, no matter what their challenge. Very tiring! But, no matter how exhausting the idea, it's disturbingly common for women to believe, at a deep or subconscious level, that everything is our fault and therefore fixing it—whatever "it" may be—is our responsibility.

Being able to let go of that exhausting belief and accept the fact that others are responsible for themselves and their lives gives us the energy and desire to be mindfully present for them in caring and compassionate ways.

As a variation of Jack Kornfield's "wisdom of insecurity," my husband, Gene, likes to use the phrase "wisdom of impermanence." One of the wonderful benefits of mindfulness is that it helps us realize the reality of impermanence and trust its ultimate wisdom, even when we don't have a clue what that wisdom will turn out to be. The greatest lessons I ever learned about the pain, grace, and wisdom of impermanence came from working with hospice. The intensity and immediacy of death, dying, and grief elicit a mindful presence. As a facilitator for grief support groups, I was awed by the courage and grace with which people dealt with loss and change. Being privy to some of the ways people rose from the ashes of grief and recreated different but nonetheless rewarding lives after the death a spouse, child, parent, or friend gave me an abiding trust in the resilience of the human spirit. Visiting with hospice patients and their caregivers, as both a therapist and a chaplain, taught me invaluable and enduring lessons about the art and joy of impermanence, letting go, and nonattachment. Not without many tears, of course, but tears are an integral part of the blessed whole of life.

Lightening Up

Feeling lighter comes naturally as a result of letting go and developing compassionate detachment for situations over which you have no responsibility or control. Lightening up also comes when you quiet your mind and establish positive and upbeat thinking habits. Although often used harshly and inappropriately, the admonishment "Lighten up!" is wise advice—advice most of us need and all of us are capable of bringing to fruition.

As we turn our attention to lightening up, mindfulness is an essential advocate. It helps us become aware of and heal the inner wounds and limiting beliefs that darken our attitudes and deplete our attributes. Being compassionately present to yourself deepens your understanding of who you really are and opens your heart and mind to the wisdom, beauty, and goodness that reside at the core of your being. Mindfulness helps you live as American Indian sage White Eagle suggests: "Be still within, be calm. Do not try to overdrive your life. Be calm, do your work quietly; live as the flowers live, opening your heart to the sunlight of God's love" (Cooke 1972).

Basking in the glow of divine love and self-love lights the fire of compassion in your heart and lightens up every aspect of your being, doing, feeling, and believing. The practice of mindfulness illumines the path to joy and well-being.

Walking Mindfully

The real wonder, Vietnamese monk Thich Nhat Hanh has said, is not to walk on water but to walk mindfully on this green earth.

✳ Breath guides you home.

✳ Mindfulness leads to a quiet mind and open heart.

✳ Compassionate inner awareness encourages self-love and acceptance.

✳ Loving-kindness toward yourself fills you to overflowing, enabling you to love others more fully and freely.

✳ Balance can be restored by mindfully focusing attention on the current moment.

✳ Simplicity facilitates serenity.

✳ Control is illusion, change is inevitable, and impermanence is immutable. Engage completely with the reality of *now*.

✳ Mindfulness helps you remember you are a remarkable, powerful, and compassionate woman.

✳ Live gently with yourself and others.

May you be mindful. May each step taken upon this beautiful green earth be blessed with compassionate awareness, gentle acceptance, and peace of mind and heart.

A few mindful moments make a world of difference.

references

Aron, Elaine. 1998. *The Highly Sensitive Person: How to Survive When the World Overwhelms You*. New York: Broadway Books.

Baraz, James. 2007. Awakening Joy (online course). www.awakeningjoy.info.

Bowen, Will. 2007. *A Complaint Free World: How to Stop Complaining and Start Enjoying the Life You've Always Wanted*. New York: Doubleday.

Buechner, Frederick. 1999. *The Eyes of the Heart: A Memoir of the Lost and Found*. New York: Harper Collins.

Chödrön, Pema. 2001. *Start Where You Are: A Guide to Compassionate Living*. Boston: Shambhala Classics.

Cooke, Grace. 1972. *The Quiet Mind*. Hampshire, England: The White Eagle Publishing Trust.

Gammons, Peter. 2007. What I learned. *USA Today*, March 7.

Lucado, Max. 2006. *Cure for the Common Life: Living in Your Sweet Spot.* Houston: Thomas Nelson.

Prather, Hugh. 2005. *Morning Notes: 365 Meditations to Wake You Up.* Berkeley, CA: Conari Press.

Siegel, Bernie. 1986. *Love, Medicine, and Miracles.* New York: Harper and Row.

Thoele, Sue Patton. 2001. *The Courage to Be Yourself: A Woman's Guide to Emotional Strength and Self-Esteem.* Berkeley, CA: Conari Press.

———. 1996. *Heart Centered Marriage: Fulfilling Our Natural Desire for Sacred Partnership.* Berkeley, CA: Conari Press.

Ware, Ciji. 2007. *Rightsizing Your Life: Simplifying Your Surroundings While Keeping What Matters Most.* New York: Springboard Press.

Sue Patton Thoele is a psychotherapist, former hospice chaplain and bereavement group leader, and author of ten books. She and her husband, Gene, live in Colorado, close to their adult children and grandchildren. Her passions include friendships, swimming with free dolphins, being a "soccer grammy," arts and crafts, exploring spirituality with her husband, and encouraging herself and others to find balance, peace of mind, and openheartedness through the gentle practice of increased mindfulness.

Her books include:

- *The Courage to Be Yourself*

- *The Woman's Book of Courage*

- *Autumn of the Spring Chicken*

- *Heart Centered Marriage*

- *The Woman's Book of Confidence*

- *The Woman's Book of Spirit*

- *Freedoms After 50*

- *Growing Hope*

- *The Courage to Be a Stepmom*

- *The Woman's Book of Soul*

- *The Courage to Be Yourself Journal*

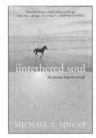